FERGUSON
CAREER BIOGRAPHIES

JIMMY CARTER

U.S. President and Humanitarian

Bernard Ryan, Jr.

Ferguson
An imprint of Infobase Publishing

Jimmy Carter: U.S. President and Humanitarian

Ferguson
An imprint of Infobase Publishing
132 West 31st Street
New York NY 10001

Library of Congress Cataloging-in-Publication Data

Ryan, Bernard, 1923–
Jimmy Carter : U.S. President and humanitarian / Bernard Ryan, Jr.
p. cm.
Includes index.
ISBN-10: 0-8160-5903-9 (hc : alk. paper)
ISBN-13: 978-0-8160-5903-4 (hc : alk. paper)
1. Carter, Jimmy, 1924– 2. Presidents—United States—Biography. I. Title.
E873.R93 2006
973.926092—dc22 2005035470

Ferguson books are available at special discounts when purchased in bulk quantities for businesses, associations, institutions, or sales promotions. Please call our Special Sales Department in New York at (212) 967-8800 or (800) 322-8755.

You can find Ferguson on the World Wide Web at http://www.fergpubco.com

Text design and composition by David Strelecky
Cover printed by Yurchak Printing, Landisville, Pa.
Book printed and bound by Yurchak Printing, Landisville, Pa.

Pages 110–124 adapted from Ferguson's *Encyclopedia of Careers and Vocational Guidance, Thirteenth Edition*

Printed in the United States of America

This book is printed on acid-free paper.

CONTENTS

1

A BAREFOOT AND SHIRTLESS BOYHOOD

On October 11, 2002, in the small town of Plains, Georgia, 78-year-old Jimmy Carter was awakened at 4:30 A.M. by a phone call. It was half an hour before his usual rising time. The call was from Oslo, Norway. The caller was one of the five members of the Norwegian Nobel Committee. They wanted Carter to know that he had just been awarded the Nobel Peace Prize. Later that day, their public announcement praised Carter for his decades of "untiring effort to find peaceful solutions to international conflicts, to advance democracy and human rights, and to promote economic and social development."

With the Nobel award came a $1 million prize and one of the world's highest honors. Carter immediately told news reporters that the award was a salute to the Carter Center, an organization in Atlanta, Georgia, that he founded in 1982. It is devoted to worldwide peace and social justice.

Jimmy Carter had then been a former president of the United States for 22 years. And getting up at 5:00 A.M. was something he had been doing for as long as he could remember. It was a natural rising time for anyone who had grown up on a farm and came from a long line of farming families.

Carters in the Land of Cotton—and Peanuts

Members of the Carter family arrived in Virginia from England in 1635 and moved into Georgia in 1780. By the 1860s and the Civil War, Wiley Carter was a well-to-do cotton farmer. His wealth, however, disappeared when the economy of the South collapsed after that war. Wiley's grandson, James Earl Carter, who was born in 1894, grew up in Plains, a town of about 600 people. There a few business buildings—a bank, drugstore, general store, barbershop, and a warehouse selling seed and fertilizer and farm and building supplies—stood on one side of Main Street. The railroad that connected Plains to Americus, Georgia, ran along its other side.

Jimmy Carter served as president of the United States from 1977 to 1981. (Library of Congress)

James Earl served in the army in World War I and then worked in the Plains Mercantile Company, a general store owned by his uncle, Alton Carter. But James Earl, who soon became known as Mr. Earl, was always willing to try something different. He ran an icehouse, then a dry-cleaning business, then his own grocery store. That store brought him such a good reputation that he was able to borrow $7,000 to buy his cherished dream: a farm.

Although Plains was a small town, it boasted an excellent hospital. A young woman named Lillian Gordy went there in 1920 to learn nursing. She and Mr. Earl met and fell in love. He insisted that she finish her training, which included six months of experience in an Atlanta hospital, before they were married on September 23, 1923. They moved into rented rooms.

Their son, James Earl Carter Jr., was born on October 1, 1924. The family welcomed his sister Gloria in the summer of 1926. Two years later, the family moved to their own house, three miles west of Plains. It stood where both the dirt road and the railroad line curved toward a village then called Archery (today it is part of Plains). The land was flat and so level that folks said, "When it rains, the water don't know which way to run."

The young Carter family was only the second white family in the small community. Some 25 to 30 others were African Americans who worked as farmhands or sharecroppers. They lived in simple shacks without running water and worked for a dollar a day (women were paid 75 cents and children earned 25 cents). The land had produced cotton for generations, but now, on most farms, peanuts were the main harvest.

White Sand and Linoleum Floors

Jimmy Carter's boyhood home was a one-story white clapboard house with porches in front and back. The yard around it was covered with white sand that the Carters often swept clean and replaced. Water came from a well they pumped by hand in the backyard, and a privy, or outhouse, stood farther back.

Indoors, linoleum covered the floors. High ceilings helped keep rooms airy in summertime. In winter, a wood-burning stove in the kitchen and fireplaces in two double chimneys gave some warmth but not enough to overcome bitter cold when it blew across southwest Georgia.

One of the few families that had telephones, the Carters shared a "party line" serving three separate homes. If the phone rang twice, the call was for them. One ring was for the Bacons, and three were for the Watsons. Everybody knew that when they answered their ring there was likely to be someone listening in another house.

No power lines reached Archery. Nighttime light came from kerosene lamps. In the Carters' living room, a lamp five feet high gave enough light for all the family to sit around it reading—an activity both parents strongly encouraged. In fact, Jimmy and his mother usually had a book or magazine in hand when they sat down to a meal. (The noon meal was dinner, while the evening meal was supper; the word "lunch" was not in the Georgia vocabulary.)

A battery-powered radio, kept in the living room and used only at night, provided such entertainment as the Jack Benny show, George Burns and Gracie Allen, Fibber McGee and Molly, or an occasional prizefight.

As soon as he was old enough to run around on his own, Jimmy knew he was free to roam the 350 acres of Carter woods and fields that stretched beyond home. From

Jimmy's boyhood home in Georgia (Library of Congress)

April to October he went barefoot and shirtless most of the time. "My most persistent impression as a farm boy," he later wrote, "was of the earth. There was a closeness, almost an immersion, in the sand, loam, and red clay that seemed natural, and constant. The soil caressed my bare feet, and the dust was always boiling up from the dirt road that passed fifty feet from our front door. . . Except during extended dry seasons, the constantly used lots for hogs and milk cows were always ankle deep in mud and manure, which made bare feet much superior to brogans."

A farm boy's life was not all carefree, however. Jimmy Carter had chores to do every day: gathering hens' eggs, pumping water, cutting firewood and stacking it, and sweeping the yard. Soon he was big enough to lug pails of water to the field hands, prune watermelon vines, and deliver slop to the hogs. He learned to pick cotton and, during hot summers, worked hour after hour alongside his father's African-American field hands. In the farm's blacksmith shop, helping his father (who was expert in using an anvil and forge), he took responsibility for turning the forge blower's hand crank at the right speed to make the charcoal burn hotly. Then, using blacksmith tongs, he held red-hot metal—a broken plow point, for example—against the anvil while his father shaped it with his hammer.

Jimmy's earliest mentor, aside from his father, was Jack Clark, the farm supervisor. He decided which farmhand would plow which field and which mule would pull each plow. He rang the giant farm bell an hour before daylight and again at noon. As a small boy, Jimmy followed him everywhere, gaining a broad education on farming and the wide world beyond the farm as he listened to Jack's never-ending commentary.

Writing years later about Jack and Rachel Clark's small house, Jimmy said, "Except in my own room in our house, this is where I felt most at home." There he played checkers and a card game called Seven-Up, and there he slept on the floor—on a mattress of corn shucks—whenever his parents were away from home.

A Five-year-old Peanut Salesman

Jimmy began selling peanuts when he was five. Loading his small wagon with peanut vines, he took them home, picked the nuts, soaked them overnight in salty water, and boiled them next morning for half an hour. They filled some 20 half-pound paper bags. Carrying them in a basket, he either walked along the railroad tracks or rode his bicycle, with the sacks in its basket, the three miles to Plains.

After selling boiled peanuts for three summers, eight-year-old Jimmy Carter had saved $125. At planting time in 1932, cotton was selling at a nickel a pound—its lowest price ever. He bought five 500-pound bales, which his father stored in a shed. A few years later, cotton prices rose to 18 cents a pound. Jimmy, not yet in high school, sold his five bales for $450. At an estate sale, he then bought five tenant houses and became a landlord. He rented two for $5 each per month, one for $2.50, and two for $2.00 and happily figured that the houses were bringing in a total of 55 cents every day. Until he went to college, he regularly rode his bike to each house each month to collect rents.

Jimmy started school in first grade just before he was six years old and not long after his sister Ruth was born. By then he could read and write. And by then Mr. Earl had made sure his son knew the rules about firearms, starting with a BB gun when Jimmy was five. Within a couple of years Jimmy had a .22 semiautomatic rifle, and by the time he was 10 he could handle his own bolt-action .410-gauge shotgun. With his father and Jack Clark he learned how to hunt quail, and at last he was allowed to go out alone with his shotgun and a farm dog. The dog pointed to a covey of birds. Jimmy flushed them and then fired. A bird dropped. Jimmy raced home to show it to his father. Mr. Earl congratulated him and then asked, "Where is your gun?" Jimmy had no idea. In his excitement, he had left it where the bird fell. It took a search party led by his father several hours to find the gun lying half concealed in a leaf pile.

By the time Jimmy was in school, his mother was widely known for her nursing skills. She served as the "family doctor," often at no charge, for countless people who could get no other medical services. The Carter home, too, was known to tramps or hoboes who, in the depths of the Great Depression, passed by on the dirt road or got off slow-moving trains in search of something to eat in exchange for doing yard work or cutting wood. Miss Lillian asked one why he came to her door but not to others'. "Ma'am, we have a set of symbols we use," he said, "to show the attitude of each family along the road. The post of your mailbox is marked to show you don't turn people away or mistreat us."

Hearing that, Jimmy and Gloria went to look at the post. They found mysterious scratches. Their mother told them not to disturb them.

Soon after starting school, Jimmy Carter decided on his future career. His mother's brother, Tom Watson Gordy, had joined the U.S. Navy at age 17 and was serving on far-off seas as a radioman. Uncle Tom sent Jimmy countless postcards, toy boats, and exotic small gifts such as a wooden box painted with dragons.

Jimmy became determined to enter the U.S. Naval Academy at Annapolis, Maryland. While still in elementary school, he wrote to the academy for a catalog and information on entrance requirements. He read and memorized the catalog until it was tattered. Before he entered high school, he read numbers of books about navy life and careers. By then the navy was, he later said, "the driving force in my life."

2

FUTURE FARMER AND MILITARY MAN

Entering Plains High School a month before he turned 14, Jimmy Carter was already a capable truck driver. At that time Georgia had no laws about drivers' licenses and Mr. Earl counted on Jimmy to run errands and deliver seed and fertilizer to the fields. In fact, when Jimmy was as young as 12, his father had let him use the pickup truck to get to dances sponsored by their Baptist church.

As he started high school, Jimmy had a baby brother, Billy, born in March 1937. With his sisters, Gloria and Ruth, getting to be big girls, he was aware that the Carters' small house was becoming crowded.

"Readers Make Leaders"

In high school, a teacher named Julia Coleman greeted Jimmy Carter. She was superintendent of Plains schools and was teaching her second generation of Plains children. She had been watching Jimmy's progress in school ever since, as a third-grader, he won a contest by reading more books than any of his classmates. Miss Coleman ran a reading club that made "Readers Make Leaders" a respected slogan. She kept track of each student's reading level and assigned books that met their mental levels. Realizing that Jimmy Carter was a self-disciplined boy from a reading family, she guided him toward poetry, art, and music.

Julia Coleman was in charge of the debating team and knew how to develop skills in logic and argument. She saw Jimmy Carter's shyness and helped him overcome it by urging him to join Friday afternoon debates. In those weekly sessions he learned how to analyze issues and express his opinions for or against them with force.

Sports were as important as books or debating. Jimmy loved baseball, but, like all farm boys, he could not stay after school for practice but had to get home to help with springtime plowing and planting. The boys played "scrub" baseball before school in the morning, at recess, at the noon dinnertime, and after school until the school bus filled. In scrub, players rotated, with the last batter moving to the outfield and all moving toward infield positions, then pitcher and catcher, until batting again. When a school bus departure or school bell interrupted, the game was suspended, and then resumed later at the same point. Jimmy Carter played in games that lasted as long as a week.

Farm work did not interfere with basketball. Slight in stature, Jimmy Carter was the fastest player on the Plains High School varsity during his junior and senior years. On getting the ball in his team's end of the court, he could be depended on to break quickly toward the opponents' end. With wintertime practice sessions, Jimmy missed his school bus and had to walk the three miles home.

While his heart was set on going to the Naval Academy, Jimmy Carter's practical mind knew he had no guarantee he would ever get there. So he took advantage of the Plains High School's strong program under the Future Farmers of America (FFA), which included more than half of the school's boys. Classroom subjects ranged from food processing to pest control to forestry and crop rotation, from caring for such work animals as horses and mules to raising milk-producing cows and beef-producing steers. Workshop classes covered welding and blacksmithing, practical carpentry, and furniture making.

A national as well as statewide organization, the FFA sponsored countless competitions that encouraged leadership in judging outstanding animals, keeping accurate records, and, in public speaking, delivering presentations. Jimmy Carter participated in all of these, and by his senior year he was an officer of the Plains High School FFA and was representing his school at national FFA conventions.

A Not-so-funny April Fools' Joke

In March 1941 all 12 boys who were seniors in Plains High School, including Jimmy Carter, planned an April Fools' joke: They would skip school on April 1 and spend the day in the town of Americus. The school principal, Mr. Y. T. Sheffield, heard of the plan. He forbade it. They went anyway, seeing a movie and stopping by the newspaper office to deliver a prepared story on their "delightful outing."

Returning to Plains, the boys were greeted by Mr. Earl, other fathers, and Mr. Sheffield with the news that for the next week each would receive a zero mark in each class. Each also received a whipping, for corporal punishment (a severe paddling of the fanny with a stiff board) was still in vogue in Georgia schools. Jimmy took the whipping ("the last one I ever had," he later said). He also went into "drydock" at home, for Mr. Earl restricted him to his home yard and fields, except for going to school, for one month.

Everyone had expected Jimmy to be named valedictorian of the Plains High School class of 1941, but the zero marks for a week reduced his final grades and he missed that honor.

The Congressman and the Dream

Jimmy and his family knew that the only way to get into either of the U.S. military academies was to receive an appointment by a U.S. senator or representative. In each of his high school years, he and Mr. Earl went to see Steven Pace, their elected congressman in the U.S. House of Representatives, while he was at home during a congressional recess. They took Jimmy's report cards along and talked about his achievements and his lifelong dedication to the dream of attending the Naval Academy. But now that he was graduating from high school, no appointment came through. The congressman advised him to wait another year and study meantime at Southwestern Georgia, a junior college in Americus.

Jimmy started as a day student, hitching rides to Americus on the Plains school bus or with friends. But studying at home was difficult, with four-year-old Billy underfoot and two younger sisters bustling about the crowded house. After the first semester, Jimmy moved into a campus dormitory. That winter, just after the

Japanese brought the United States into World War II by bombing Pearl Harbor, he made the college's "all-star" basketball team. He worked as a laboratory assistant and was elected vice president of the freshman class and runner-up for the title "Mr. Southwestern."

Again Jimmy and his father called on Congressman Pace, and again they were disappointed. But as they were leaving, Pace said he could give Jimmy an interim appointment for September 1943. It would depend on his completing science courses not available at the junior college.

Jimmy transferred to Georgia Tech in Atlanta as a general engineering student, taking courses recommended by the Naval Academy. He joined the naval ROTC, studying required courses in military science, navigation, and seamanship. In each of three semesters, he stood in the top 10 percent of his class and was listed on the honor roll.

In the last week of June 1943, Jimmy and a boy from Americus took the Silver Meteor train from Plains to Washington, D.C., and then found a bus to Annapolis. On June 28, reporting for duty as a midshipman, Jimmy Carter weighed 121 pounds. Ahead of him, under the academy's wartime program, was an accelerated agenda that would require him to do four years of academic and naval study in only three years.

From Plebe to Ensign

A boy who had been rising before dawn all his life had no trouble bouncing out of bed at the Naval Academy's 6:15 A.M. reveille. But Jimmy Carter did refuse to submit to one Annapolis tradition. With upperclassmen permitted to inflict hazing on the plebes (the word used for freshmen), he was ordered to learn and sing "Marching Through Georgia," the Civil War song of William Tecumseh Sherman's army. It was a humiliation traditionally imposed on any plebe from Georgia. Jimmy refused.

As punishment, for several days plebe Carter had to eat his meals while holding himself in sitting position just above, but not touching, his chair. At the same time, he was forced to "eat square meals," which meant lifting his fork straight up from his plate to the level of his mouth, then bringing it directly to his face.

Jimmy kept a diary during his first year at Annapolis. In it he recorded many instances of hazing: the endless pushups and trots around the running track even before reveille, or an upperclassman's suddenly smacking him with a broom or, at the table, with a serving spoon.

Smiling had long ago become Jimmy Carter's way of dealing with any difficult person or situation. But a smiling plebe was not what an Annapolis upperclassman wanted to see. "My main trouble," Jimmy confided to his diary, "was that I smiled too much." When passing a group of seniors,

Jimmy's class portrait from the U.S. Naval Academy in Annapolis, Maryland (Associated Press)

he wrote, "I soon learned to concentrate on a serious subject." And, he added, he learned how to "wipe off" a smile.

Life at the Naval Academy was not all hazing and discipline. In athletics, Jimmy Carter played on the under-140-pound football team, was considered an outstanding cross-country runner, and proved he was a skilled high jumper and pole vaulter on the track team. On the firing range, plebe Carter showed he was adept at handling weapons, an activity that came naturally to a young man who had been using guns since he was five.

In the classroom, Jimmy was surprised to find that, academically, his Georgia Tech grind had been tougher than that of Annapolis. In the dorm, during what little "free time" they had, he and his roommate, Bob Scott, who had trained as a classical pianist before getting his appointment to Annapolis, played recordings of the world's musical masterpieces. Sundays saw Jimmy maintaining his own hometown tradition: teaching Sunday school in a nearby Baptist church.

Polishing Decks and Manning an Antiaircraft Gun

During the summer of 1944, Jimmy Carter got a taste of the real war that was raging across the Atlantic and Pacific oceans. He and others were assigned to a training cruise aboard the USS *New York*, an elderly battleship in the Atlantic Ocean.

Directed by the ship's regular crew, they "holystoned" decks—polishing them with a white brick—and rotated through duties that taught them all aspects of operating the ship. During battle-station alerts, which were frequent, Jimmy's permanent assignment was the operation of a 40-millimeter antiaircraft gun. He was also permanently assigned the care of a "head," or toilet, that had a habit of overflowing.

Warnings of German submarines, which were ranging along the east coast of America, brought evasive and turbulent zig-zagging. The cruise ended with a rush trip home for repairs after something—an uncharted reef, perhaps, or a passing torpedo (no one ever knew which it was)—knocked a blade off one of the ship's four propellers. That handicap made each zig and zag a violent, shuddering experience for all aboard.

One requirement for midshipmen was that they learn to recognize the silhouette of every German and Japanese ship and airplane. In drills, they got only a split second to look at each one. Jimmy's naval professors knew they could count on him to identify them instantly.

The Girl at the Picnic

Before his training cruise in the summer of 1945, Jimmy went home in July for a brief leave. His sister Ruth invited a friend named Rosalynn Smith to a family picnic. Rosalynn was a shy 17-year-old who had just completed her freshman year at Georgia Southwestern College. Strong in science and mathematics and also a first-team basketball player, she had been valedictorian at her Plains High School graduation.

Rosalynn liked the way the 20-year-old midshipman teased her, and together they went to a movie that evening with Ruth and her boyfriend. On the way home, riding in the rumble seat of Ruth's boyfriend's car, Jimmy surprised Rosalynn by kissing her—something she had never let a boy do on a first date. Then, at home, Jimmy surprised his mother by saying, "She's the girl I want to marry."

Jimmy Carter was on his training cruise in the North Atlantic when President Harry S. Truman announced on August 6, 1945, that a U.S. plane had dropped an atomic bomb on Hiroshima, Japan. On August 14, after another such bomb had leveled Nagasaki, the Japanese agreed to surrender. The war was over. Jimmy Carter and many thousands of American sailors and soldiers realized they would not have to participate in the bloody invasion of Japan for which they had been training.

At home on Christmas morning 1945, Jimmy had a special gift for Rosalynn: a silver compact engraved "ILYTG." The letters stood for "I love you the goodest," a phrase used secretly within the Carter clan. A couple of days later, before returning to Annapolis, he proposed. Much as she loved him, Rosalynn said no, for she was determined to finish college. They agreed to keep the proposal secret. Then in February, over Washington's Birthday weekend, Rosalynn visited Annapolis with Miss Lillian and Mr. Earl, and she and Jimmy quietly began planning their wedding.

By the end of his senior year, midshipman Carter had earned a record for excellence at the Naval Academy. He had not, however, emerged as a leader. As one classmate put it, "A big man on campus he was not." Another classmate recalled, "He was very well liked by his company. But he was a loner. He went out of his way to be perhaps more friendly to more people, but he didn't need other people's close bond of friendship to support his own ego and personality—he had a very strong character."

At the Naval Academy graduation, one of the high points was always the moment when each officer's shoulder boards were pinned to his uniform by his closest female relative. In June 1946, Rosalynn Smith pinned one of Ensign Jimmy Carter's shoulders while his mother pinned the other. Then on July 7, in the Methodist church in Plains, the Carter family and a few close friends saw the bride, in a white-and-blue dress with a corsage of purple-throated orchids, and the groom, in a naval officer's white summer uniform, become Ensign and Mrs. James Earl Carter Jr.

Wonderful Training and Terrible Duty

New graduates of Annapolis had to serve at sea for their first two years and were assigned to ships by lottery. Jimmy drew the USS *Wyoming*, a battleship built in 1911, before World War I. It was considered so unsafe that it was allowed to sail only in Chesapeake Bay from its base in Norfolk, Virginia. There, testing new equipment for use in gunnery, fire control, radar, navigation, and communications, it roamed the navy's gunnery practice area. While his 19-year-old bride waited in their apartment in Norfolk, Jimmy was at sea from Monday through Thursday of every week for a year. He later said the experience aboard the *Wyoming* was "wonderful training" but "terrible duty."

On July 3, 1947, Jimmy and Rosalynn welcomed their son John William Carter (whom they called Jack) into the world. Jimmy was able to get two weeks' leave and did cooking, laundry, and baby care to help Rosalynn. Then his Chesapeake Bay duty continued as the *Wyoming* was decommissioned and replaced by the USS *Mississippi*, an equally decrepit vessel.

After almost two years of such "terrible duty," Jimmy applied for a Rhodes scholarship, a possibility open to naval officers. He came in a close second. A student of Elizabethan poetry won the scholarship.

Disappointed but not discouraged, Jimmy applied for the navy's submarine service, the highly selective and most prestigious branch that used only volunteers. Overjoyed that he was accepted, he and Rosalynn and Jack moved in June 1948 to New London, Connecticut, for submarine officers' training school.

The training was hard work in the classroom every morning and at sea each afternoon, submerging, resurfacing, and resubmerging in Long Island Sound and firing dummy torpedoes in mock battles. Fifteen percent of the class flunked out, but Jimmy stood third among the 52 submariners who graduated in December. He was assigned as electronics officer aboard the USS *Pomfret*, a vessel based at Pearl Harbor, Hawaii, that was scheduled for a three-month cruise to China.

Rosalynn and little Jack stayed in Plains while Jimmy drove to Los Angeles, flew to Honolulu, and sailed into the vast Pacific Ocean on December 30. Within a week, the *Pomfret* met seas that were the raging opposite of pacific as a tum-ultuous storm—said to be one of the worst in that ocean's history—sank seven ships.

Rosalynn Carter (Library of Congress)

While violently seasick for a week, Ensign Carter never failed to fulfill his duty to stand watch. One night, as all submarines then had to do every 24 hours, the ship was surfaced to recharge its batteries despite the storm. Jimmy was outside on the bridge when a giant wave smacked him. It ripped his grip from the handrail. Entirely detached from his ship, he swam within the wave. It deposited him atop the five-inch gun 30 feet from where he started.

After Jimmy's three-month tour to ports along the China coast, Rosalynn and Jack moved to Hawaii. The young family spent the next 18 months enjoying life in a two-bedroom navy apartment at Pearl Harbor, with Jimmy alternately on sea or shore duty. In their spare time he learned to play the ukelele and she learned to hula dance. He took advantage of the navy's excellent hobby shops to practice his woodworking skills and learn cabinetmaking.

As the end of Jimmy's tour in Hawaii drew near, two major events occurred. On April 12, 1950, Rosalynn gave birth to James Earl Carter III, whom the hospital nurses nicknamed "Chip." And on June 27 President Truman ordered U.S. air and naval forces to support South Korea against the invasion by North Korea that had begun two days earlier.

New Lieutenant and New Ship

By now, Jimmy Carter had been promoted from ensign to lieutenant j.g. (junior grade). Because he had earned outstanding ratings, he was selected to go to New London, where the navy's first postwar submarine, the K-1, was being built. For several weeks before and after the launch of the K-1, Jimmy was the only navy man aboard and worked closely with the sub's naval architects and engineers.

Test runs of the K-1, with a full crew and with Jimmy Carter as engineering officer, proved it could stay submerged for weeks at a time. They found that lowering or raising the periscope only a few inches could make the ship sink or rise. "This fine balance," Jimmy wrote afterward, "took a lot of skill, experience, and luck, but gave us a platform of almost complete silence from which to listen to our prospective targets. We would hear all kinds of strange sea creature sounds and could detect ships at extraordinary distances."

One of the submarine's crewmen later described Lieutenant Carter's calm disposition during terrifying moments of the test runs: "I can remember him being in a really precarious situation a couple of times . . . the ship would be sitting almost vertical. He'd just laugh and scratch his head and say, 'You know, there's something wrong, we just shouldn't be this way.'"

In a sense, submarine discipline was one of Jimmy Carter's mentors. Life in the restricted space of the giant capsule below the sea's surface called for perfect performance by each member of the crew. Everyone depended on everyone else. The atmosphere encouraged a certain confidence on Jimmy's part that his shipmates could sense and return. The experience taught him how leadership is expressed by example and is achieved through cooperation with those being led.

On June 1, 1952, Jimmy was promoted to full lieutenant and the demanding position of executive officer of the

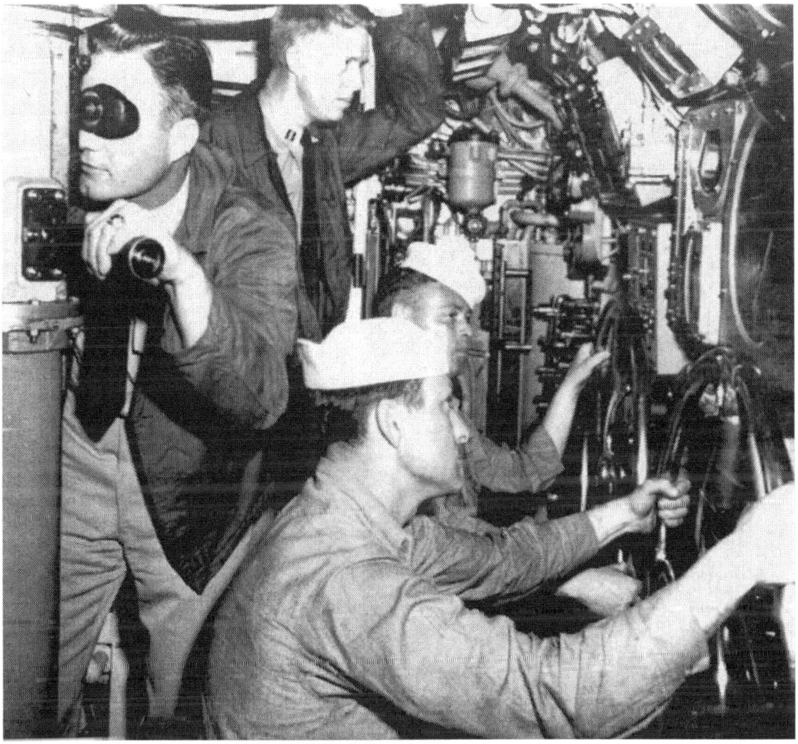

Jimmy (standing, facing right) aboard submarine USS K-1 in 1952. During this time Jimmy worked on a U.S. Navy program to build atomic submarines. (Associated Press)

K-1. Life ashore was equally demanding, for on August 18—Rosalynn's birthday—a third Carter baby boy, Donnel Jeffrey, was born.

Busy as he was with the K-1 test cruises and family life, as well as woodworking at home, Jimmy Carter applied himself to gaining his rating as a submarine commander. This required that he write a thesis. He developed a guidebook on a new system of underwater rangefinding that used passive listening tools. The devices and his guidebook were soon employed widely by the navy.

Creating Underwater Atomic Power

Qualified for command, Jimmy heard about a new program headed by a navy captain named Hyman Rickover. It was to build two atomic-powered submarines, and it demanded officers who had top-notch engineering experience and technical skills. Jimmy applied for it. He faced a tough interview with Rickover himself, who was well known for the strong-willed, hard-fighting, and self-confident way he had pushed the nuclear-power program through the government's Bureau of Ships and the Atomic Energy Commission.

Rickover grilled Lieutenant Carter for two hours on everything from music to seamanship, from literature to naval tactics and electronics. "He always looked right into my eyes," Jimmy later wrote, "and he never smiled. I was saturated with cold sweat."

As Jimmy joined Rickover's program in the fall of 1952, he and Rosalynn and their three boys moved to Schenectady, New York, where the General Electric Company was building the first seagoing atomic power plant. Jimmy was the senior officer handling details of the precommissioning of the *Sea Wolf*, including training noncommissioned officers in basic reactor technology and its math and physics. To get hands-on practice, they worked in a mock-up of a nuclear submarine.

Jimmy Carter later described working for Rickover. "He had a profound effect on my life, perhaps more than anyone except my own parents," he said. "He was unbelievably hardworking and competent, and demanded total dedication from his subordinates. We feared and respected him and strove to please him. I do not in that period remember his ever saying a complimentary word to me. The absence of a comment was his compliment. He scared me."

Before the *Sea Wolf* was launched, 29-year-old Jimmy learned early in 1953, in a call from his mother, that his father was dying of cancer of the pancreas. He went home to see Mr. Earl.

3

FROM PEANUTS TO POLITICS

During 11 years away from home except for brief visits, Jimmy Carter had not realized how respected and beloved Mr. Earl had become. His seed and fertilizer warehouse business was prosperous. He owned more than 5,000 acres of farmland. He had recently been elected to the Georgia state legislature. Hundreds of people, from sharecroppers to shopkeepers, knew that he treated everyone fairly regardless of skin color, and every farmer knew that Mr. Earl would let him buy on credit while waiting for the crops to come in. Now, Jimmy learned, an entire community was deeply concerned about his father's terminal illness.

Facing a Tough Decision

Jimmy's mother, Miss Lillian, made it clear that she wanted him to come home and take over the family business. She had always concentrated on nursing, not on crops and warehousing, so she was not fit to take control. Gloria and Ruth, like most southern daughters at the time, had not been raised to take responsibility for the family enterprise. Billy, just 16 years old, was too young to take charge.

Jimmy and Rosalynn talked it over. Jimmy was the navy man he had always hoped and expected to be. He was getting good assignments and enjoying the work. Rosalynn liked the navy life, for it gave her special status and freed her from the strict social structure in Georgia. But in Plains some 1,500 people depended on the Carter warehouse and the Carter peanut farm for their weekly pay. Both Rosalynn and Jimmy had their roots in Plains, where lifelong friendships were stronger than the good but briefer military friendships that changed every couple of years when assignments changed.

The more Jimmy thought about it after Mr. Earl died a few weeks later, the more he said to himself (as he later wrote), "God did not intend for me to spend my life working on instruments of destruction to kill people." He called his mother and said, "I have no alternative. I am coming home."

Rosalynn was not happy with Jimmy's decision. Nor was Rickover, who expected total loyalty from anyone he had admitted to the new world of nuclear-powered submarines. But on October 9, 1953, Jimmy Carter received his honorable discharge from the U.S. Navy.

Arriving back in Georgia, the Carters found that a yearlong drought had severely reduced the peanut crop. The dry spell continued through 1954. Farmers could not pay back loans Mr. Earl had advanced. Jimmy had to extend the loans.

Drought, Debt, and a New House

Jimmy and Rosalynn and their three boys lived in a small apartment in a public housing project. The former navy lieutenant discovered he could not get a $10,000 loan at a local bank. He took courses to bring his knowledge of agriculture up to date. As the rains resumed in 1955 and peanut vines flourished, he joined temporary workers in the backbreaking job of weighing and shipping tons of peanuts. At the same time, as Rosalynn began keeping the books and processing the billing, she discovered that she was an ace bookkeeper and accountant. "I loved it," she said later. "To make all those books balance? I liked it better than anything I had ever done."

Over the next several years, Jimmy Carter built up a prosperous peanut business. He expanded the warehouse operation to include a three-acre plot for storing peanuts, a peanut-drying system, and a peanut-shelling mill. He also spent countless hours helping his community. He headed a project

After the death of his father, Mr. Earl, Jimmy took over his family's peanut farming business. (Getty Images)

to beautify Plains, obtaining grants to help pay for paving the streets. He organized farmers and contractors to donate time, equipment, and skills to build a 35 x 75-foot town swimming pool. He served on the hospital board, the library board, and the school board, where he soon became chairman.

Meantime, cultural changes were sweeping across America. On May 17, 1954, the U.S. Supreme Court's decision in *Brown v. Board of Education* declared that segregation in public schools was unconstitutional. In Georgia, the White Citizens Council began signing up white males to fight against the integration of the schools. Some of its members stopped in at the Carter warehouse and told Jimmy he was the only local white man who was not a member of their group and that his business could suffer if he did not join. They said they would pay his $5 dues for him. Saying "I would as soon flush $5 down the toilet," he refused to join.

As a result of Jimmy's forthright decision, the Americus Country Club expelled the Carter family, but the Carter business lost only two customers. And by 1961, Jimmy and Rosalynn were having a simple modern brick ranch-style house built on their own plot on a shady street near the center of Plains.

Not Afraid to Fight the System

Another cultural change came on March 26, 1962, when the U.S. Supreme Court struck down a voting system that had been in place in the south since soon after the Civil War. Under that system, an entire county could cast a single "unit vote" in an election. In effect, because local courthouse politicians decided how the county would vote, the vote of the man in the street did not count. Now the Supreme Court, in *Baker v. Carr*, said the rule had to be "one man, one vote." Its decision was the first significant step in giving voting rights to black citizens, who had not previously even been allowed to register to vote.

Jimmy Carter was busier than ever that summer and fall. Through the harvest season, he and Rosalynn worked alongside their employees and ate and slept at the warehouse, going home only to shower and change clothes. But he kept thinking about that "one man, one vote" decision and about the civil rights movement that was spreading across the south. Then, on his birthday, October 1, he learned that, in the primary election just two weeks away, no one from his county was running to represent the seven counties of Georgia's southwest district in the state senate.

That day, Jimmy announced his plan to run. Rosalynn immediately designed a poster and business cards. Disc jockeys interviewed him on the radio. Newspapers ignored him. On election day he visited each county courthouse and voting precinct. A friend who was hanging out at one as a poll-watcher found that ballots were being torn up by a party boss who substituted other ballots that he marked himself. That precinct had just 410 registered voters, but when the polls closed the count showed 420 votes—yet, from its book of 500 ballots, only 333 had been used.

When the entire district was counted, Jimmy lost the primary fight by 139 votes. He decided to appeal to the County Democratic Executive Committee for a recount. It failed to act. Meantime, a petition signed by 10 percent of the county's registered voters declared that voting not only in this senate race but in previous races had been fraudulent. Jimmy appealed to the State Democratic Committee. Arguments batted back and forth for 48 hours until a superior court judge ruled the day before the election that no names could appear on any ballots; it would be a write-in election. Jimmy Carter won it, 3,013 votes to 2,182.

Voters across Georgia began to hear about Jimmy Carter, the state senator who never gave up. "If I have one political attribute as the cause of my success," he later said, "it would be tenacity. Once I get onto something I am awfully hard to change."

Great Accomplishments in 45 Days

Jimmy Carter served in the Georgia state senate for four years. The legislature was in session only 45 days a year, mostly in the winter months, when he was least needed at the warehouse in Plains. While he was in Atlanta, Rosalynn was in full charge of the business and ran it well.

During his time in Atlanta, Senator Carter became known for his dislike of such special-interest groups as insurance-company executives, bankers, paving contractors, and even doctors when they lobbied against proposed bills that could improve public health. In the 1964 legislative session, he was appointed to a special commission to examine education in Georgia. Its work resulted in the legislature's providing increased funding statewide for education and the upgrading of Georgia Southwestern from a two-year curriculum to four years. He was also invited to join the Executive Committee of the State Democratic Party, where he was assigned to a task force rewriting the party rules.

Step by step, Jimmy Carter was becoming known to more key people and broadening his political base. He helped establish the West Central Georgia Area Planning and Development Commission. As its permanent chairman, he led it as it introduced Neighborhood Youth Corps and Head Start programs. Under his leadership the commission also created tourist attractions that improved area business by restoring the Andersonville Civil War prison, a Creek Indian village, and an antebellum mansion.

By the time he returned to Atlanta in January 1966, Jimmy Carter had made up his mind (though he told no one except Rosalynn and his immediate family) to run for the U.S. House of Representatives that fall. He was well known across Georgia's Third Congressional District. On the Appropriations Committee he held a seat every senator wanted. He had fought hard to reduce taxes on small rural school districts. Fellow legislators in Atlanta had voted him one of the five most effective senators. Capitol reporters had put his name in nomination nationwide as one of the 35 outstanding lawmakers in America.

On March 3, 1966, Jimmy Carter announced he was running for Congress. He and Rosalynn began a careful campaign, county by county, that was punctuated daily by informal speeches and hand-shaking anywhere and everywhere. Then in May everything changed. The leading candidate running for governor had a heart attack and dropped out. Jimmy's chief opponent for the seat in Congress, Bo Callaway, declared he would run for governor instead. Jimmy busily tried to find someone to oppose Callaway for governor. Finding no takers, on June 12 he announced that he himself would run.

Shortly thereafter, Jimmy Carter met two new friends who were to play major roles in his political life. One was Hamilton Jordan, a college student who impressed Jimmy when they met in Albany, Georgia. Jimmy made him youth coordinator for the campaign. The other was a North Georgia bank president named Bert Lance, who admired Carter not only for his ambition to improve life for Georgians but also for his strong religious faith. He became a zealous supporter.

These two came aboard only 10 weeks before Primary Day on September 15, which in Georgia was the same as election day: Any Democrat who won the primary was sure to win the election.

A Change in Attitude

In the September 1966 election for governor of Georgia, Jimmy Carter did not win. By then, six candidates were on the ballot, and Carter came in third. No one had a majority, so a runoff election was held. It, too, failed to show a majority winner. That meant, under the Georgia Constitution, that the State House of Representatives had to elect the governor. It chose Lester Maddox, a well-known politician who believed strongly in the segregation of races.

Jimmy told his supporters he would run again in 1970. However, his deep disappointment was destroying his self-confidence, and he felt sure he faced another defeat. "I did not get much pleasure out of success or victories," he later said, "and I felt personally responsible for all the small failures and defeats. I had very little genuine interest in other people and I was quite disconsolate and dissatisfied with myself."

Jimmy's sister Ruth guided him into a change in attitude. She had recently become a born again Christian in the Baptist faith. As she later recalled, she told him, "You've got to be willing to accept God's will, Jimmy, no matter what He should want you to do."

Jimmy had been a Bible reader and a Sunday school teacher since his youth, but now he gave fresh thought to religion. He studied the works of Reinhold Niebuhr, a theologian who had written popular books that taught the relationship among politics, Christianity, and overall moral values. He became convinced of Niebuhr's good sense in warning that a nation's pride could turn to arrogance and in advising that any country show humility in its worldwide relationships.

While Jimmy and Ruth were holding long discussions about religion, their mother, who was bored with Plains and with running a small nursing home, joined the Peace Corps. Upon signing up for a program to teach nutrition in India, she learned the Hindi language. Then she found that volunteers were needed to teach family planning in Maharashtra, so she learned to speak Marathi. By the end of 1966, she was busy with a new life halfway around the world. Describing the experience after 18 months in India, she wrote home:

> I didn't dream that in this remote corner of the world, so far away from the people and the material things that I had always considered so necessary, I would

> discover what Life is really all about. Sharing yourself with others, and accepting their love for you is the most precious gift of all.
>
> If I had one wish for my children, it would be that each of you would dare do the things and reach for goals in your own lives that have meaning for you as individuals, doing as much as you can for everybody, but not worrying if you don't please everyone.

It was a message that her son would carry with him for a long time to come.

Meantime, Jimmy was planning the 1970 campaign for governor and welcoming a new arrival at home, for on October 19, 1967, Rosalynn gave birth to Amy Lynn, a daughter for whom she and Jimmy had long hoped. Amy's brother Jack was 20, Chip was 17, and Jeff was 15.

"I'm a Peanut Farmer from Georgia"

In May 1968 Jimmy took 10 days off from working on his campaign for governor. He and three other men met in Lock Haven, Pennsylvania, a coal-mining town of 37,000. Representing the Southern Baptist Home Mission Board, they went in pairs, knocking at 10 to 15 homes each day. When a door opened, Jimmy said, "I'm a peanut farmer from Georgia," and related how he and his companion were witnessing for the Lord.

"The whole week," Jimmy said later, "was almost a miracle to me. I felt the sense of the presence of God's influence in my life. It was a new sense of release and assurance and peace with myself and a genuine interest in other people that I hadn't experienced before."

Developing his plans for the campaign, Jimmy hired Hamilton Jordan to handle increasing piles of campaign mail, then named him campaign manager. Next he hired Jody Powell, a 26-year-old graduate student in political science who had written a perceptive paper on Alabama segregationist governor George Wallace. He was soon not only Jimmy's regular driver and personal assistant but also the center of his inmost political circle, for he and Jimmy found they thought alike on every political issue.

A third key member of the Carter team was advertising man Gerald Rafshoon, who turned the humble peanut into a campaign symbol, with pro-Carter men wearing gold peanut pins on their lapels while the ladies enjoyed the glamour of gleaming peanut necklaces and bracelets. A Rafshoon TV commercial showed the candidate on his farm harvesting peanuts while the soundtrack said, "Can you imagine any of the other candidates for governor working in the hot August sun? No wonder Jimmy Carter has a special understanding of the problems facing everyone who works for a living. Isn't it time someone spoke up for you?"

Primary day was September 9. In a vote the *Atlanta Journal* called the most stunning upset in years, Jimmy Carter won 48.6 percent while his opponent, Carl Sanders, got 37.7 percent. In a runoff on September 23, Jimmy's majority of the Democratic votes rose to 60 percent. In the November election, 60 percent of all Georgia voters elected Jimmy Carter their governor.

"The Time for Racial Discrimination Is Over"

Governor-elect Jimmy Carter wrote his own inaugural speech. Few Georgians expected the simple strong words of the eight-minute address he delivered on January 12, 1971. Many were stunned when they heard their just-sworn-in governor say, "At the end of a long campaign, I believe I know our people as well as anyone. Based on the knowledge of Georgians north and south, rural and urban, liberal and conservative, I say to you quite frankly the time for racial discrimination is over. No poor, rural, weak, or black person should ever have to bear the additional burden of being deprived of the opportunity of an education, a job, or simply justice."

Nationwide, no one expected a statement like that from a Georgia politician. It marked a major step forward in the ongoing march of the civil rights movement. *Time* magazine, with Jimmy's picture on its cover, gave its readers an ardent appraisal of Governor Carter, saying he represented the "New South" and contrasting him with Alabama's Governor Wallace.

His four years in the Georgia Senate and the four years he had spent preparing for and running for the governorship had convinced Jimmy Carter that what Georgia needed most was a complete reorganization of state government. As soon as he was elected, he had proposed saving some $50 million a year by cutting the number of state agencies from 300 to 22. Once in office, he replaced longtime officeholders who were in jobs because of party connections rather than merit. He appointed Jody Powell as his press secretary, Hamilton Jordan as his executive assistant, and Bert Lance, who had proved to be an inexhaustible campaign fund-raiser, as state highways commissioner.

Those who kept an eye on the capitol in Atlanta soon realized they had a governor who liked his job. He was at his desk by 7:15 every morning. He expected his staff people to be on time and he liked to work with them directly—not in group meetings, which he hated, nor through supervisors. They soon discovered his sponge-like eagerness to know every detail of every project. When he held a press conference, they knew they could count on him to demonstrate that he knew more about the subject than any reporter asking questions.

During his first year in office, Jimmy concentrated his energy on the government reorganization plan. By

January 1972, it filled a 2,500-page presentation book describing 300 proposed changes. Some 65 agencies in the state budget would be reorganized into 20 agencics. For example, separate departments that had each covered housing, physical and mental health, drug treatment, welfare, and parole and probation would join in the Department of Human Resources. In the judicial system, which had not been reformed in 75 years, the governor would no longer be allowed to appoint judges whether or not they were qualified. Now a Judicial Selection Commission would consider candidates and decide on the five most competent for the governor to choose from.

A Man Like a South Georgia Turtle

From his own experience in the Georgia General Assembly, Jimmy knew that getting his reorganization plan approved by the House and Senate branches would not be easy. Countless groups and individuals wanted no changes made at all. Support for the plan had to be created, and for that Jimmy authorized a statewide Public Awareness Program. It included printing many thousands of brochures, producing audio tapes and films—in which Jimmy himself appeared—for radio and TV broadcasts and hosting hundreds of conferences and luncheons at the capitol and the governor's mansion.

Georgia governor Jimmy Carter in 1971 (Associated Press)

By the time the legislature convened for its 1972 session, Governor Carter's determination was widely known. Georgia Secretary of State Ben Fortson put Jimmy's reputation into words while testifying before the Senate Committee on Economy, Reorganization, and Efficiency in Government. "Don't pay attention to that smile," he said. "That don't mean a thing. That man is made of steel, determination, and stubbornness. Carter reminds me of a South Georgia turtle. He doesn't go around a log. He just sticks his head in the middle and pushes and pushes until the log gives way."

On February 21, the last day on which the law permitted the General Assembly to meet, bitter arguments and negotiations over the final bill continued into the evening. The bill passed, with 198 of its 243 proposals approved, as the clock struck midnight.

Looking toward Washington

Under the Georgia Constitution, the governor must leave office at the end of one four-year term, so Jimmy Carter knew in early 1972 that he had only three years to go in the Atlanta capitol. He also knew that 1972 was a national election year. He thought about the Democrats who were trying to win the nomination to run against Republican President Richard M. Nixon: Senator George McGovern, Senator Henry "Scoop" Jackson, Senator Edmund Muskie, and Alabama's Governor Wallace. And he knew he thought none of them outstanding.

The Democratic National Convention in Miami presented an opportunity for Jimmy Carter to become better known nationwide. He accepted an invitation to deliver the nominating speech for "Scoop" Jackson, and he became known as the leader of the "Stop McGovern" movement. Nonetheless, McGovern won the nomination.

By mid-October, Jimmy's advisers—including Jordan, Rafshoon, and Peter G. Bourne, a medical doctor and anthropologist who had branched into politics—met with him and said they were convinced that the inevitable re-election of President Nixon would end McGovern's political career. They urged Jimmy to start planning immediately on a run for the presidency in 1976.

The group was frank in also urging him to work on overcoming some imperfections they perceived. They knew Jimmy was dynamic and forceful in discussions with individuals or small groups but not in making speeches to large audiences. On television, he seemed weak. His knowledge of such areas as economics and foreign affairs needed considerable broadening.

The governor listened and smiled and made no commitment. But on the day after Nixon's victory he called together the same group, along with Bert Lance and two or three others, to talk about 1976. He asked Hamilton Jordan to draft a four-year plan for gaining the Democratic nomination.

Jimmy began speaking to such audiences as the National Press Club in Washington. There he talked so skillfully about national problems and the Nixon administration's failure to understand people's needs that Georgia Congressman Andrew Young jotted on his place card, "Damned if he's not running for president."

Jimmy Carter was still far from being a household name across America. That became clear when in the spring of 1973 his staff people got him an appearance on a leading TV show, *What's My Line?* On it, he answered from behind a curtain while a panel, trying to guess what his job was, asked questions. None of them figured out that their guest was the governor of Georgia.

Gaining Friends and Knowledge Worldwide

By May 1973 Jimmy was in Europe on a mission ranging from England to Israel to promote trade with Georgia businesses, including meeting with West German Chancellor Helmut Schmidt to discuss the possible construction of a Volkswagen plant in the governor's state. The trip gave Jimmy insight he had never before had in foreign affairs and economics.

Next, multimillionaire and banker David Rockefeller appointed Jimmy to the Trilateral Commission, a new group that included academic, business, and political leaders from North America, Japan, and Western Europe. They met twice a year to discuss and suggest solutions to problems such as world population, the Middle East, the international monetary system, or the laws of the sea. Jimmy seized this opportunity to study the various issues before the commission. The depth of his knowledge soon impressed its members.

Over the next two years, Jimmy Carter continued building his reputation among powerful leaders and with the general public. At the unveiling of a portrait of Dean Rusk, a Georgia native and former U.S. secretary of state, a speech by Democratic leader and Massachusetts Senator Ted Kennedy was, as Jimmy said later, "basically the same speech I was going to make." Jimmy then made a spontaneous speech that attacked the judicial system for its failure to protect the common citizen. The staid audience of prominent Georgians was stunned. "It was a defining speech in Carter's career," wrote one commentator, "embodying his deepest beliefs and values, and his rationale for being involved with politics."

Meantime, key events that were to affect Carter's future were occurring:

- The Watergate scandal broke, charging top White House people up to and including President Nixon with obstructing justice.
- Ted Kennedy, who had long been a strong contender for the Democratic nomination for president in 1976, announced that he would not run.
- Vice President Spiro Agnew resigned in a tax-evasion scandal dating from when he was governor of Maryland. Nixon appointed Michigan Congressman Gerald R. Ford to replace him.

- The Democratic National Committee made Jimmy its campaign chairman for the 1974 midterm elections, giving him nationwide exposure to party leaders.
- Nixon aide John D. Ehrlichman and others involved in the Watergate break-in were found guilty of conspiracy to violate civil rights, and the U.S. Supreme Court ruled that Nixon had to release 64 tape recordings of White House conversations.
- Saying Nixon was "the worst president in my lifetime," Jimmy Carter became the first state governor to call for his impeachment.
- Facing impeachment, Nixon resigned and Ford took office as president.
- In the November 1974 elections, Democrats gained wide majorities in both houses of Congress and increased state governorships from 32 to 36.

During this tumultuous time in U.S. history, Jimmy Carter had campaigned in 32 states, making friends with candidates and young party workers. On December 12, 1974, he formally announced his candidacy for president of the United States.

4

THE ROAD TO THE WHITE HOUSE

Despite his appearance on the cover of *Time*, and despite his many months of day-and-night work campaigning for Democrats across 32 states, the name Jimmy Carter was relatively unknown to most Americans in 1975. People who heard that the governor of Georgia was running for president asked, "Well, what has he done?"

Wide Range of Accomplishments

Carter supporters could recite a long list of his administration's accomplishments. In education, Governor Carter had raised teachers' pay, added special-education teachers, and improved teaching in early childhood development. He had also made sure poorer counties received education funding equal to that given to richer counties, and he had improved financial aid for college students.

In health matters, he had provided full funding for a program of testing and research to end sickle-cell disease. A statewide network of treatment centers for drug abuse and improved laws dealing with first-time drug offenders had been established, and medical care for preschool children had been improved. The governor had also installed community mental health centers statewide and started a program called "Cripplers and Killers," to recognize and cut down the major causes of disability and death.

Under Jimmy's leadership, Georgia had passed some of the toughest environmental protection laws in America. It had taken special tax advantages away from big companies, adding $28 million a year to the state treasury. It had given 18-year-olds full voting rights. And it had opened offices in Canada, Belgium, Germany, Brazil, and Japan to produce international trade for Georgia businesses; in fact, in 1973 alone, Japanese manufacturers had invested $125 million in Georgia factories.

Jimmy's successor as Georgia governor was inaugurated on January 13, 1975. Now Carter could spend his full time campaigning. The peanut warehouse was well managed and needed little of his attention. He and Jody Powell headed for Washington on January 15 for dinner meetings with political leaders and an interview session with the editorial board of *The Washington Post*. Afterward, one of its members, Bob Maynard, who was African American, said, "I was not expecting much, but was enormously impressed."

Smiles and Home Visits

Jimmy crisscrossed the nation throughout 1975. He spoke to small groups and large. He flew tourist class and stayed not in hotels but in private homes—even the most humble—so he could learn voters' genuine concerns and build a network of their friends and relatives. Meeting Hispanic farm workers, he spoke Spanish. Workers at factory gates and shoppers in shopping centers found his warm smile greeting them, his hand outstretched, as they came and went.

The smile, the charm, and the sincerity came through to Americans who had been disillusioned by the lies and deceit foisted on them by their elected officials during the Vietnam War and in the Watergate crisis. And as he met individuals and groups and they sensed his integrity, Jimmy in turn sensed two basic points: how greatly the public was concerned about the mismanagement of the federal government and its need for reorganization and how strongly people felt that basic values had to be re-established.

While he was working nationwide to make friends and get his name better known, Jimmy Carter had to keep building up two aspects of his strategy for winning the Democratic nomination. The first was financial. His backers were not wealthy. A new law resulting from Watergate, however, said the federal government would match funds that eligible candidates raised if those funds came to at least $5,000 in at least 20 states—and if the $5,000 minimum resulted from individual contributions of $250 or less. It took the Carter workers until August 18 to qualify for the matching funds.

The second strategic problem was how to get the majority of the 3,071 delegates to the 1976 convention to vote for Carter. Primary elections or caucuses—closed meetings of party members—would pick delegates, so it was important to enter every primary, starting with Iowa's caucus on January 19. This meant campaigning in one state after another as their primary election days came along.

One of the key people in the primary campaigning was Rosalynn Carter. Starting in April, she set out—along with her son Jack's mother-in-law, Edna Langford—in her Chevrolet on a cross-country odyssey that covered 42 states. She rang doorbells, successfully invited herself to make speeches at all-male Rotary Clubs, visited courthouses (where she knew the political hangers-on were sure to gather), and insisted on front-page attention in newspapers ("Don't let them fob you off," she later told campaigners, "to the society editor or the women's page.").

She even got a cattle auctioneer to interrupt his spiel and let her speak to his crowd.

By autumn, money was tighter than ever. Hamilton Jordan and other leading staffers worked without pay for three months. But on October 27 a *New York Times* political reporter named R. W. "Johnny" Apple changed things when his story headlined "Carter Holds Strong Lead Going Into Iowa Caucuses" appeared on his paper's front page. Countless other stories on Jimmy Carter's campaign had appeared in hundreds of papers, but Apple enjoyed a certain respect among newsmen that others only longed for. Immediately, Jimmy found that TV news cameras were assigned wherever he went. He could hardly keep up with the requests for interviews. Best of all, campaign contributions began rising significantly.

The Peanut Brigade

In a national election year, the Iowa caucus is always the earliest. The candidate who wins in Iowa gains a head start on all others. Nobody expected Jimmy Carter to capture 29.1 percent of Iowa Democrats, but he did so on January 19, 1976, with his nearest opponent getting only 11.4 percent. The victory put his picture on the covers of both *Newsweek* and *Time*, made him an instant celebrity, and prompted party contributors to start sending big checks.

Next was Mississippi, where Carter won only 14 percent of the vote while Alabama's Governor Wallace took 44 percent. Jimmy then won by a narrow margin in Oklahoma, came in a close second in Alaska, and won in Maine.

Like Iowa, New Hampshire is a key state in a national primary race. Carter workers who thronged there long before its February 24 voting day had become known as his "Peanut Brigade," and *Newsweek* had quoted one New Hampshire Democrat as saying, "If that many people thought that much about him to come all the way up here, then he must be a good man." The voters gave Carter a strong victory with 29.4 percent of the ballots.

Two weeks later, on March 9, trouncing Alabama's Wallace, Jimmy won the Florida primary. A week after that, he won Illinois, his first victory in a northern, industrial state. On March 31, however, Senator Henry "Scoop" Jackson won Massachusetts. Wisconsin and Pennsylvania became Carter states in April. May brought victories in Texas, Georgia, Indiana, the District of Columbia, Michigan, Nevada, Tennessee, Kentucky, and Arkansas but losses in Nebraska, Maryland, Idaho, and Oregon. In June he lost in California and New Jersey but won in Ohio.

As he campaigned, often near exhaustion, in state after state, Jimmy knew he had to convince African-American voters that he was the Democrat who could win the White House. On June 1, at the Martin Luther King Jr.

Hospital in Los Angeles, he gave what many consider his finest speech of the campaign. Paying honor to King as "the conscience of his generation," Jimmy said: "He was the man who gazed upon the great wall of segregation and saw that it could be destroyed by the power of love. I sometimes think that a southerner of my generation can most fully understand the meaning and the impact of Martin Luther King's life." The speech ended strongly: "I see an American president who does not govern by vetoes and negativism, but with vigor and vision and affirmative leadership, a president who is not isolated from our people, but feels their pain and shares their dreams and takes his strength from them. I see an America in which Martin Luther King's dream is our national dream."

By mid-June, with the Democratic National Convention due to open on July 12 in New York City, Jimmy was sure of nomination on the first ballot. He chose Senator Walter "Fritz" Mondale of Minnesota as his running mate.

Next, Jimmy worked with his speech writer on his acceptance speech, starting with his own 25-page draft on yellow legal paper and telling the writer, "I want to use words that people down in Plains can understand." He also made sure the writer did not refer to the American public as "they," as so many politicians did, but rather as "we." "I am one of the American people," he told his writer.

When he delivered the speech at the convention, Jimmy's first words were those he had said for nearly four years to everyone who opened a door when he knocked: "My name is Jimmy Carter and I'm running for president." The delegates rose, cheering and stomping as tears flooded their eyes. Their enthusiasm kept rolling as their candidate concluded: "It is time for America to move and to speak, not with boasting and belligerence, but with a quiet strength—to depend in world affairs not merely on the size of an arsenal but on the nobility of ideas—and to govern at home not by confusion and crisis but with grace and imagination and common sense."

Campaign, Debate, and Victory

Now Jimmy had two tasks to handle at the same time. He had to campaign even harder to win the election than he had campaigned to win the nomination. At the same time, presuming he was going to win, he had to grasp, in incredible detail, America's situation both within its borders and worldwide. The week after the convention, he was briefed in three all-day meetings with experts who had served in prominent national and international positions. They covered three broad subjects: national security and defense, economics, and worldwide economics and foreign policy.

Wherever he went, Jimmy Carter now found reporters with notepads in hand and TV crews alongside.

Jimmy and his vice-presidential running mate, Walter Mondale, wave to the crowd at the Democratic National Convention in New York, 1976. (Getty Images)

The journalists seemed astounded to discover that this presidential candidate could come out of a six-hour meeting, announce "Here's what I learned today," and give them a detailed summary of everything that had been discussed.

Three debates between Jimmy Carter and President Gerald Ford were held, with each television audience estimated at 100 million. Jimmy later admitted that during the first 20 to 30 minutes of the first debate he was in awe of the presidency and could not think of Ford as an equal. Then, he later said, "I relaxed and enjoyed the rest of the debate, and realized that he was running for president the first time, like I was, and that he was the nominee of his party, as I was, and although he was the incumbent, that, as far as the debate went, we were equals, and once I removed that reticence and treated it as a contest, I didn't feel ill-at-ease or nervous anymore."

The second debate was on foreign policy. Asked about the Helsinki Accords, in which the Soviet Union and the United States agreed to notify each other of military maneuvers, Ford astonished the debate audience by blurting that "there is no Soviet domination of Eastern Europe and never will be under a Ford administration." In truth, much of Eastern Europe was under Soviet influence at the time.

The debate moderator asked Ford to clarify his statement. He made it worse. "I don't believe that the Yugoslavians consider themselves dominated by the Soviet Union," he said. "I don't believe the Romanians consider themselves dominated by the Soviet Union. I don't believe the Poles consider themselves dominated by the Soviet Union."

Ford had bungled a major foreign policy question. Jimmy Carter pointed out that the Soviet Union was then maintaining 20 military divisions, including 300,000 troops, in those Eastern European countries. "I would like to see Mr. Ford convince the Polish-Americans and the Czech-Americans and the Hungarian-Americans in this country," said Jimmy, "that those countries don't live under the domination and supervision of the Soviet Union behind the Iron Curtain." Ford's blunder put Carter 45 percent ahead of him in a public poll asking who won the debate.

The voting on November 2 was so close that nobody knew the election's outcome until well into November 3. Jimmy and Rosalynn Carter waited in an Atlanta hotel until 3:30 A.M. before the final count in Mississippi clinched Jimmy's victory. He went to speak to his crowd of exhausted supporters, then on to Plains. Dawn broke as the Carters arrived. They were greeted by "When the Saints Go Marching In" played by the lively high school band from Americus, and they found hundreds of townspeople—who had waited all night for them—cheering and clapping their hands in wild exuberance.

5

PRESIDENT CARTER

Inauguration Day, January 20, 1977, was bitterly cold. President Jimmy Carter delivered his inaugural address from high on the Capitol steps. Then he and Rosalynn got into the president's armored limousine to lead the inaugural parade. As the car entered Pennsylvania Avenue, it stopped. Jimmy and Rosalynn got out. Following a suggestion made earlier by Wisconsin's Senator William Proxmire, a physical fitness buff, they walked the mile to the White House hand-in-hand, leading the parade.

Pardon for Draft Dodgers

President Jimmy Carter's first official act the next morning was to fulfill a promise he had made while campaigning. He signed an executive order granting amnesty—in effect, a pardon—to most Americans who had evaded the draft to avoid serving in the Vietnam War. White House phone lines immediately jammed with calls from furious Americans who considered the pardon disrespectful to Vietnam veterans. The new president, however, felt confident that forgiveness could help heal one of America's severest wounds.

Jimmy surprised Washington experts by not appointing a chief of staff. Who, they wondered, was to set his priorities and organize each day? Who would, in effect,

Chief Justice Warren Earl Burger swears in Jimmy as the 39th president of the United States while Rosalynn looks on. (Getty Images)

guard the door of the Oval Office and let in only those whose business was so important that only the president could make decisions on it? It took a while for Washingtonians to understand what Jimmy meant when he said, "I never have wanted to have a major chief of staff between me and the people who worked for me. I have always wanted to have a multiple like seven or eight or maybe as many as ten people who had direct access to me all of the time without having to go through an interim boss."

Among those who had such direct access were most of the members of the president's cabinet (that is, his official advisers), who were appointed by him and who headed the main departments of the government. One of them, Attorney General Griffin Bell (head of the Department of Justice), commented on Carter's method: "You would have had absolute chaos if he had not been so intelligent and had he not worked twelve hours a day. He made everything come through him, but he was very proud of his system."

Jimmy brought Hamilton Jordan to the White House as his principal assistant but did not name him chief of staff. He made Jody Powell his press secretary. Bert Lance came in as director of the Office of Management and Budget. Soon senators and congressmen on Capitol Hill as well as the staffers in the White House knew that President

Carter maintained a closer friendship with Lance, a convivial, well-liked extrovert, than with anyone else. Lance dropped in almost daily and seemed to be an adviser on every issue.

Americans observed other differences in their new leader. Here was a president who sold the presidential yacht *Sequoia* and who refused to have "Hail to the Chief" played when he appeared in public. His daughter, Amy, was a student not in a private school but in a District of Columbia public school. His staff was told to get rid of unneeded TV sets and limousines. And when Jimmy Carter headed for the Marine helicopter on the south lawn, he carried his own suit bag.

The new first lady brought surprises, too. In cabinet meetings, Rosalynn joined White House staffers taking notes but not speaking. From the outset, as her special area of interest, she concentrated on helping the mentally ill. At her insistence, Jimmy created, by executive order, the Presidential Commission on Mental Illness and Mental Retardation.

Agenda: From Energy to Foreign Policy

President Carter arrived in the Oval Office with a wide variety of proposed improvements that he expected Congress to legislate. He wanted authority to reorganize the executive branch of the government. He hoped for laws to control the cost of hospital care and to reform the welfare system. A consumer-affairs agency, a bill to define ethics in government, a reorganization of the administration of Social Security—all were on his agenda.

Especially important in the new president's plans was an extensive energy program. Right on cue came a bitter-cold winter that severely strained energy supplies. Jimmy put on a cardigan sweater and sat before a fireplace on February 2 to tell the national television audience about the energy crisis. He promised to create a new Department of Energy at the cabinet level and, within 90 days, send Congress a broad program to reduce the nation's consumption of energy and its use of imported oil and to develop new sources of energy at home.

The public admired Jimmy's so-called fireside chat. It reminded oldtimers of radio talks given by President Franklin D. Roosevelt. But getting any bill through Congress is not easy. Jimmy assumed that everybody on Capitol Hill would understand how a strong energy program would help the nation. Unfortunately, his energy bill's trip through Congress was slow.

Soon after his election, Jimmy had concentrated on one of the major challenges that he knew he would face: U.S. foreign policy. Consulting with his top advisers, he decided to pay special attention to one country—Panama—and to one area on the far side of the globe—the

Middle East. At the same time, he let Soviet premier Leonid Brezhnev know of his interest in human rights and in reducing weapons.

Panama's situation appealed to Jimmy Carter's sense of fairness. It had lived since 1903 with a treaty that kept the Panama Canal under the control of the United States. That treaty, he said, represented "morally questionable aspects of past American foreign policy." It was time, he said, to give the Panama Canal to Panama.

It was also time, the president believed, to settle the longstanding feud between Israelis and Arabs. He asked his advisers to revive an earlier conference on the Middle East that had been co-chaired by the Soviet Union and the U.S. Planning for it, during the spring of 1977 he welcomed to Washington such leaders as Israeli Prime Minister Yitzhak Rabin, Crown Prince Fahd of Saudi Arabia, King Hussein of Jordan, and President Anwar Sadat of Egypt, and he met in London with Syria's President Hafex al-Assad.

At the same time, Rosalynn Carter was actually in charge of American foreign policy in Latin America during an extensive trip. In Jamaica, Costa Rica, Colombia, Peru, Ecuador, Venezuela, and Brazil, she talked seriously with government heads on such subjects as oil prices and control of the drug trade. Her successful tour astounded people in the U.S. State Department and in Congress who

Rosalynn and Jimmy Carter and their family, 1976 (Getty Images)

had always thought first ladies should simply make smiling goodwill tours of schools and hospitals.

No Canal and No Bomber

In the summer of 1977, two of the president's major programs were put in place. On August 4, after extensive wrangling, both the House and Senate passed the bill establishing the new Department of Energy.

In September, Panamanian president Omar Torrijos Herrera came to Washington to sign two treaties. One transferred control of the canal from the U.S. to Panama after the year 1999. The other gave the United States the right to maintain military defense of the canal. The treaties were controversial. Many accused Carter of "giving away the canal," but others recognized that he was completing negotiations that previous White House administrations had developed and that the treaties were typical of his sense of fairness.

The president made another controversial decision during his first summer in office. On June 1, he canceled the Pentagon's plan to build a new bomber, the B-1. The departing 1976 Congress, which had to approve such a major expense, had left it to the incoming president to decide. Carter said it was "a waste of money. We did not need it strategically, and I thought the technology was too expensive for what we got."

The Lance Affair

The summer of 1977 brought President Carter a major headache that soon became known as "the Lance Affair." When Bert Lance took the job as director of the Office of Management and Budget, he had $3.3 million worth of stock in the National Bank of Georgia. He agreed to put the stock in a blind trust. That meant that he would have no control over it while he was in office, and those taking care of it would be required to sell the stock by the end of 1977. By July, however, the stock's value had dropped to $1.7 million. Lance, who was working in the Carter administration for much lower pay than he had received as president of the Georgia bank, was in financial trouble.

President Carter asked the Senate Government Operations Committee to extend the deadline for his best friend, Bert Lance, to sell the stock. The request caused reporters to search Lance's background. One *New York Times* columnist suggested that Lance had gained a $3.4 million loan from a Chicago bank by peddling his influence. Then the controller of the currency issued a 394-page report that said that, while Lance had done nothing illegal, he had engaged in "unsafe and unsound banking practices." At the Georgia bank, it reported, Lance had allowed bank officers and their relatives to run up large overdrafts.

Lance delivered an impressive two-hour statement to a hearing of the Government Operations Committee and handled dozens of tough questions. However, Vice President Mondale, Senate Majority Leader Robert Byrd, and all Carter's advisers agreed that Lance should resign. He did so on September 21.

The resignation deprived Jimmy Carter of his strongest supporter and adviser since he began running for office as governor. For years, when somebody came to him with a problem, he had been able to say "talk to Bert about that" and it would be solved. Now, he knew, those days were over.

6

PEACEMAKER

Jimmy Carter's first concern in the fall of 1977 was how to make peace between Egypt and Israel. When Egyptian president Anwar Sadat visited Washington the previous spring, he and Carter had become good friends. Now in mid-November, at the suggestion of the American president, Sadat told the Egyptian parliament that, if invited, he would visit Jerusalem. Israeli prime minister Menachem Begin responded quickly by asking Carter to forward an invitation to Sadat. On November 20 Sadat made history by addressing the Israeli parliament, also known as the Knesset.

In December, Begin visited Cairo and Carter visited Tehran and met with the Shah of Iran, calling him "an island of stability" in the troubled Middle East. The American president was laying the groundwork for one of his administration's major accomplishments.

Getting Congress to Approve

Meantime, Carter kept pushing to get Congress to act on various items on his long agenda. He was authorized to appoint 148 new judges. He cut out the regulation of airline fare rates. He signed a bill prohibiting strip mining, another bill launching the $13.7 billion Housing and Community Development Act, and another reducing and simplifying taxes. His plan to reorganize the executive branch of the government was approved. And, although Republican opponents called it "the biggest peacetime tax increase in U.S. history," Congress approved a new Social Security proposition that was expected to keep the system solvent until 2030.

Jimmy Carter was especially satisfied with a decision he made on April 7, 1978, when he canceled production of the newly developed neutron bomb. It could produce only a small blast and little heat but would release a massive wave of radiation that could penetrate heavy armor or several feet of earth. "The average American," he said, "even peanut farmers, can understand the difference between a weapon that destroys property and one whose penetrating radiation is basically designed to kill human beings."

Speaker of the House Tip O'Neill saluted the president's judgment and also recalled his decision to cancel the B-1 bomber. Carter, he said, was "the only president who doesn't have to rely on the Pentagon to make his military decisions."

The Summit at Camp David

In the spring, Secretary of State Vance had held meetings in England with the prime ministers of Egypt and Israel but found it impossible to reach any understandings. Vance now agreed with the president, who had long said that a peace plan would have to be generated by the United States. Carter decided to take an extremely bold step: Rather than following the usual method of having staff people from each side draw up preliminary agreements for the heads of state to review, he would get the leaders themselves to negotiate, with the help of their advisers, in a summit conference. He knew he faced a giant risk, for if the summit meeting failed to produce peace he would get all the blame. He handwrote invitations to Camp David, the quiet presidential retreat in Maryland's northwestern Catoctin Mountains, for Vance to deliver in person to Sadat and Begin.

The Camp David Summit began on September 4, 1978. For the next 13 days, Jimmy Carter worked back and forth, sometimes alone with either man, sometimes with both, sometimes with their staff people. To keep the atmosphere informal, they adjourned meetings to play tennis, take walks, and visit the nearby Gettysburg Civil War battlefield. Some discussions lasted until after midnight. The main issues they debated were the return of the Sinai Peninsula from Israel to Egypt and Israel's annexation of the West Bank area from Palestine.

Often Jimmy Carter thought the talks, which were frequently vehement if not actually angry, would end in disaster. On the 11th day, Vance found Sadat packing his bags to leave. Jimmy Carter, threatening to end their personal friendship, got him to stay. Next day, after endless arguments over the West Bank, Begin agreed to let the Knesset answer the question: "If agreement is reached on all other Sinai issues, will the settlers be withdrawn?" Sadat accepted Begin's agreement. In the White House at 10:15 the next evening the three leaders signed both the Framework for Peace in the Middle East and the Framework for the Conclusion of the Peace Treaty Between Egypt and Israel.

Describing Carter's work at Camp David, *The Wall Street Journal* said the president's "inspired leadership" and "brilliant success" had "re-established his presidency in fundamental terms." *The Washington Post* considered the summit meeting "a first, big step toward realizing the promise of his presidency."

Not the Traditional Politician

Anyone who was watching the Carter presidency knew that the Camp David summit succeeded because Jimmy Carter hated to fail and refused to give up. It worked

Egyptian prime minister Anwar Sadat, Jimmy Carter, and Israeli prime minister Menachem Begin shake hands after signing plans to forge peace in the Middle East. Jimmy was insstrumental in bringing the two leaders together. (Library of Congress)

because he had faith in establishing reconciliation and trust between opposing sides. Yet it was, as the signed documents said, only a "framework" and, as the *Post* said, only a "first, big step."

As President Carter's second year in office drew to a close, those who worked with him—from Vice President Mondale on down—had all come to realize that their leader was not a traditional politician. He did not consider the presidency a political office. When a decision had to be made, Jimmy expected it to be made strictly on the merit of the subject. If it was the best thing for the country as a whole, he felt, it should be approved—with none of the give-and-take, negotiations, or compromises of politics.

The president had to face strong criticism from his own party in December 1978 when 2,500 Democrats held a "mini-convention" in Memphis, Tennessee. It passed a forceful resolution censuring Carter for making hefty cuts in social welfare programs in order to balance the budget. In a rousing speech, Senator Ted Kennedy advised the president that nothing since the Vietnam War had divided the party as severely as the budget cuts he planned.

December brought Jimmy Carter two other matters to wrestle with. China was one, and the Camp David Summit was the other.

On December 15, the president announced that on January 1 the U.S. would diplomatically recognize the People's Republic of China, a step President Nixon initiated. Nevertheless, most Republicans, led by Arizona Senator Barry Goldwater, were furious, especially over a planned visit to America by China's deputy prime minister, Deng Xiaoping. Few saw that setting up normal relations with China would help maintain a balance against the Soviet Union, which was always eager to control the countries west of China from Pakistan to Turkey.

The Camp David "framework" for peace had called for formal signing by December 17, but that deadline passed. Both Sadat and Begin, once they were back home and facing their parliaments, had had second thoughts. Sadat felt he had gained too little, and Begin felt he had yielded too much. In fact, he had already infuriated Arab leaders by announcing plans to build new settlements on the West Bank.

On March 8, the president and first lady flew to Egypt. Sadat said, "Brother Jimmy, I will do whatever you think is best." Armed with Sadat's agreement, Carter went to Israel and met with Begin's cabinet officers and the 25 members of the Knesset's Foreign Relations Committee. As a result, on March 26, 1979, on the White House lawn, Sadat and Begin shook hands and signed their historic treaty. The moment was, critics and friends agreed, a remarkable triumph for President Jimmy Carter.

A Nation Out of Gas

On the homefront, the energy crisis would not go away. Over the July 4 weekend, drivers in the greater New York City area found nine out of 10 gas stations closed. So did 80 percent of Pennsylvania drivers and half of those in Rhode Island. Next, furious truckers who could not get fuel blocked expressways in Levittown, Pennsylvania, causing two nights of violence that injured 100 people and brought 170 arrests.

Jimmy Carter asked speech writer Pat Caddell for words on the gasoline shortage. Caddell argued that polls proved that America had heard all it wanted to hear about the energy crisis. He advised the president to speak about how the nation had lost its self-confidence.

Vice President Mondale looked at Caddell's ideas for the speech and rejected them outright. Over many months, the vice president had become convinced that the president himself, along with his staff, did not understand how much the American people looked to their leader for solid solutions to problems.

Advice from the Vice President and Others

On the July 4 weekend, the Mondales joined the Carters at Camp David. There, while the two men strolled on the grounds, the vice president told the president that Caddell's speech could doom him politically. Then Mondale, speaking from the genuine friendship the men had developed, advised the president that he needed to rethink his entire attitude about the presidency.

Jimmy Carter listened. He kept listening for the next eight days as he invited some 150 people—congressmen and governors, labor leaders and economists, businesspeople and religious leaders, names well-known and unknown—

to Camp David to chat with him. By his own later estimate, he spent 90 percent of his time listening. Slowly but surely, Jimmy realized that he had been occupied 24 hours a day with personally managing the government and its foreign policy rather than providing the leadership that people longed for. He also learned from these meetings that he needed to improve his relations with the press and replace some members of his cabinet. And he knew from polls that his approval ratings were at an all-time low.

The country felt that Jimmy Carter was a weak president. He had spent most of his time managing the small details of his government, of the legislation he wanted put through, and of the foreign policy he expected to improve world situations. He had not, however, coped with the broader problem of how a president leads by setting goals for the country and by putting his officials in charge of achieving them.

When Carter spoke to the country on Sunday evening, July 15, he used some of Caddell's ideas as he described America's current "crisis of confidence." "Our people are losing faith," he said, "not only in government itself but in the ability as citizens to serve as the ultimate rulers and shapers of our democracy." Then, saying, "Energy will be the immediate test of our ability to unite the nation," he demonstrated leadership by presenting the six points of a clear blueprint for coping with the energy crisis.

House Speaker Tip O'Neill called Carter's speech "one of the strongest and best he has made." The president's approval rating rose from 26 to 37 percent.

Following up on the eight-day meetings, the president asked all members of his cabinet and staff to resign. He then announced which resignations he would accept, resulting in 34 departures. And to take charge of running the White House, he appointed Hamilton Jordan as his chief of staff.

During the fall of 1979, Carter proposals won approval. The Department of Education was established. Middle-income college students gained financial assistance. The Elementary and Secondary Education Act increased funding for schools. Welfare reform received $5.7 billion. The ailing Chrysler Corporation received $3.7 billion in aid (the automaker repaid it all within a few years). Regulations controlling communications, banking, and the rail and trucking industries were removed.

Perhaps most important, Congress passed the six-point energy bill. It led to establishment of world prices on natural gas and crude oil, and it provided tax credits for those who conserved energy and used insulation and for research and development in solar energy.

The public, however, was still doubtful about Jimmy's presidency. A Harris poll in September reported that 70 percent of the country believed he could not win re-election. A week or so later, at lunch with Jimmy and Rosalynn, Senator Ted Kennedy told the president that for the sake of the Democratic party and of the country he would run against him in 1980.

The Hostage Crisis

Meantime in Iran, the Shah Mohammad Reza Pahlavi, a dictator who had been supported by the U.S. since 1953 because he controlled the rich oil resources of his country, was facing real opposition for the first time. The Shah and Empress Farah had visited the White House and had become friends of Jimmy and Rosalynn when the Carters visited Tehran in December 1977. Now the Shah's countrymen wanted him out. With his military forces failing to control demonstrations and strikes, the Shah fled in September, first to Egypt, then Morocco, then Mexico. A fundamentalist religious leader, the Ayatollah Khomeini, took charge.

October brought Jimmy Carter the news that the Shah was seriously ill with non-Hodgkin's lymphoma. Many influential people in the government requested that President Carter admit the Shah for treatment in U.S. hospitals.

Carter thought hard about that. In a meeting, with Mondale present, he asked, "Does somebody have the answer as to what we do if the diplomats in our embassy are taken hostage?"

No one responded. "I gather not," said the president. "On that day we will all sit here with long, drawn, white faces and realize we've been had."

On October 23, Carter gave permission for the Shah to come to New York for treatment at the Sloan-Kettering Institute. On November 4 in Tehran, some 3,000 militant student demonstrators, outraged that America had wel-

Iranian Shah Mohammad Reza Pahlavi and Jimmy Carter in 1977; Jimmy's friendship with the Shah incited the Iranian hostage crisis, which lasted until the end of his presidency. (Getty Images)

comed the Shah, mobbed the U.S. Embassy. They seized 66 hostages.

Two days later, on November 6, Senator Kennedy announced his candidacy for the next Democratic nomination for president.

Carter ordered two Navy task forces, each with an aircraft carrier, into the Persian Gulf. He also froze all Iranian assets in the U.S. and ended all oil purchases from Iran. The militants then released 13 hostages but kept the other 53. In the White House, planning for a rescue mission began.

On December 4, Jimmy Carter formally announced that he would run for re-election. The American public—infuriated over Iran's holding U.S. hostages and pleased with Carter's response to the crisis—raised his approval rating from 32 percent to 61 percent.

As December ended, the Soviet Union invaded Iran's neighbor, Afghanistan, to put its preferred Afghan leader in charge. Retaliating, Carter stopped all sales of American grain to the Soviet Union and then canceled plans for American athletes to participate in the summer Olympic games in Moscow. He also—with great regret but determined to face up to the Soviet challenge—asked the U.S. Senate to set aside its plan to ratify the SALT II Treaty, which would limit U.S. and Soviet production of nuclear weapons.

Another Election and a Disaster

On January 21, 1980, Jimmy Carter beat Senator Ted Kennedy in the Iowa primary to decide on the next Democratic nomination for president. Two days later, he delivered his State of the Union speech to Congress and the nation. In it he addressed everyone's worry that the Soviet invasion of Afghanistan might be a first step toward its gaining a warm-water port on the Indian Ocean or capturing some of the oil wealth on the Persian Gulf. "Any attempt by any outside force to gain control of the Persian Gulf region," he said, "will be regarded as an assault on the vital interests of the United States of America." Remembering the Monroe Doctrine, in which President James Monroe in 1823 declared that the U.S. would not allow European interference in the Western Hemisphere, many people called Carter's position "the Carter Doctrine."

Now came other primary elections. Carter beat Kennedy in New Hampshire, Florida, and Illinois but lost in New York and Connecticut. Meantime, on April 7, President Carter let the National Security Council at the United Nations know that he planned a rescue mission to free the U.S. hostages in Iran. The military joint chiefs of staff and Vice President Mondale were confident the mission would be successful. Only Secretary of State Vance, who himself had long worked with the Defense

Department, disagreed. "I'll guarantee you something will go wrong," he told Mondale. He threatened to resign if the mission failed.

The disaster occurred on April 24 as eight helicopters flew from the carrier *Nimitz* to rendezvous south of Tehran with six C-130s that held the rescue team. One helicopter got lost in a sandstorm. Two broke down with mechanical problems. Another crashed into a C-130 on the ground. Eight servicemen died. Four others were severely burned. No hostages were rescued.

As commander-in-chief, President Carter took full blame for the mission's failure. Secretary Vance resigned and was replaced by Senator Edmund Muskie.

Nominated Versus the Actor and Governor

By the time of the Democratic National Convention, Jimmy Carter had gained enough delegates to win his party's nomination for president. (Senator Ted Kennedy did not quit the race until the second night of the convention.) Meeting in July, the Republicans nominated Ronald Reagan, a former Hollywood actor and former California governor, for president. Reagan was a man who, unlike Carter, always appeared to be certain about how to solve any problem. Often his solutions were impractical and left his underlings to work out details, but he had an uncanny ability to convince people he was right. His personality—smiling and self-assured—contrasted with Jimmy Carter's soul-searching introspection and concern with managing details.

Reagan had a way of making people feel good. He launched his campaign with the optimistic slogan, "It's morning in America." His speeches let people know he wanted to shrink the government that, he said, imposed on them everywhere. "The American people wanted simple, short, black-and-white answers," said one commentator. "Carter's honesty compelled him to ambivalence and gray areas. He acknowledged the complexity of modern life and Reagan didn't."

With the election campaign going on, the White House learned early in September that the Iranian government was willing to discuss releasing the hostages.

Final Days in Office

One of the high points of the campaign was a TV debate between the candidates on October 28. Jimmy was well prepared, but he was not aware that Reagan's advisers had managed to obtain a copy of the president's secret briefings on national defense and foreign policy. With this inside information, Reagan appeared self-confident in discussing various issues. At the same time, he conveyed a sense of superiority, saying, for example, "There you go again" when Carter made points that could reveal his opponent's incompetence. Opinion polls revealed that the public saw Reagan as the winner.

Reagan was indeed the winner on November 4. Of the low voter turnout (only 52 percent of registered voters showed up at the polls), Reagan captured 51 percent versus Carter's 41 percent. Analysts said that half the ballots were cast against Jimmy Carter rather than for Ronald Reagan and that traditional Democrats had stayed home, refusing to vote for either man.

Carter invited the president-elect to the White House for an hour long briefing on the major issues facing him. Reagan asked no questions and took no notes, but at the end he asked the president for a copy of his notes to give his staff.

With two and a half months to go in office, Carter went back to work, keeping a close eye on continuing negotiations over the Iran hostages and pushing two key bills through Congress. One created a $1.6 billion superfund for cleaning up toxic waste at chemical dumps. The other nearly tripled America's total wilderness land and more than doubled the area of national parks.

As Inauguration Day neared, President Jimmy Carter made a farewell speech from the White House. "In a few days I will lay down my official duties in this office," he said, "to take up once more the only title in our democracy superior to that of President, the title of citizen."

Negotiations now showed that release of the hostages also seemed near. Jimmy was ready to fly to Germany to greet them and return for Reagan's swearing-in, but nothing happened. At dawn on January 20, 1981, President Carter got word that papers releasing the hostages had been signed.

7

HUMANITARIAN AND NOBEL LAUREATE

Home again in Plains, Jimmy and Rosalynn Carter set about fixing up the house they had scarcely occupied for 10 years. They also faced a major financial problem: Their warehouse, which had been held in a blind trust while they were in Atlanta and Washington, D.C., was more than $1 million in debt. However, publishers were making enticing offers for both Jimmy's and Rosalynn's memoirs. The couple began writing. Jimmy, in fact, soon piled up 6,000 pages of notes to work from. And to free their minds from business distractions, they sold the warehouse operation to the giant Archer-Daniel-Midland Company.

In October 1981, the Carters received the startling news that Egyptian president Anwar Sadat had been assassinated by fundamentalist Muslims—that is, Muslims who believe in literal interpretations of the Koran—in retribution for making peace with Israel. Representing the U.S. at his funeral in Cairo was his friend "Brother Jimmy," along with former U.S. presidents Nixon and Ford.

A Place to Help Resolve Disputes

Jimmy Carter was aware of an American tradition that had developed in his lifetime: the construction of giant libraries to house the files and keepsakes of former presidents. Already there was talk of raising $25 million for such a showplace. He did not like that idea. He wanted something different and more purposeful. One night he sat up in bed and awakened Rosalynn, saying, "I know what we can do with the library. We can develop a place to help people resolve disputes."

Jimmy's idea grew out of his experience at Camp David. He envisioned a center where those who opposed each other—whether nations or blocs within a nation—could meet to argue, propose compromises, and settle their disputes. Not even the United Nations offered such a concept.

Over a few weeks, the idea grew quickly. Rosalynn and Jimmy saw its possibilities for helping to control nuclear arms and establish peace, for developing improved services in healthcare, for broadening the recognition and defense of human rights, and for relieving suffering and hunger among needy people worldwide. They made sure the plan included a basic ground rule: For any dispute to be settled, all parties involved had to participate and do so with full trust in all the others.

The Carter Center was formally founded in 1982 in partnership with Emory University in Atlanta, where Jimmy had been appointed a "distinguished professor." To build its headquarters and install its staff, $10 million was raised at dinners in major American cities, and still more millions came from business leaders worldwide.

A President in Jeans and T-shirt

While all this was going on, Jimmy somehow found time to write *Keeping the Faith: Memoirs of a President*, which was published in 1982. That fall, he took a strong interest in a worldwide organization headquartered in nearby Americus. Habitat for Humanity was dedicated to enlisting volunteer workers to build or repair homes for needy people anywhere from Georgia to Indochina and Africa. The idea appealed to Jimmy and Rosalynn's deep Christian faith. They soon agreed to help Habitat with its fundraising.

The Carter Center, which Jimmy and Rosalynn founded in 1982, promotes humanitarian causes and peaceful resolution of conflicts. (AFP/Getty Images)

In the fall of 1983, Jimmy faced family sorrow. He lost his sister Ruth to pancreatic cancer, the same disease that had killed his father. Then his mother, Miss Lillian, died a month later. In his determined way, Jimmy kept working. One day in March 1984, Jimmy arrived at a new Habitat house under construction in Americus. There he put his carpentry skills to work helping to frame in the building. That exhilarating day led him to organize a busload of 36 volunteers from among his church and other friends for a week's work in New York City in September. Over five days, all hands including Jimmy and Rosalynn—by now a competent carpenter herself—framed windows and doors, laid new floors, and mounted sheetrock in a dilapidated six-story building at 742 East Sixth Street that was home to 19 families. At night, all slept in bunk beds in a Baptist church.

Journalists who traipsed along reported their astonishment at seeing an American ex-president working and sweating in jeans and T-shirt. The publicity helped make Habitat famous and brought in not only thousands of volunteers but some $10 million in donations. By December 1986, 171 U.S. communities and 17 other countries had Habitat projects under way, and Jimmy Carter was beginning to realize how far-reaching the influence of an ex-president could be. He promised to spend at least one week a year laboring with hammer and saw for Habitat. Expressing his admiration for its achievements, he said, "I've had many experiences in my life and in Christian work, in business, government, and politics. I've traveled almost everywhere in the world, and I do not know of anything I've seen that more vividly illustrates love in action than Habitat for Humanity."

A Worm in the Water

Over the next several years, Jimmy Carter seldom sat still. He wrote and published a book, *The Blood of Abraham*, on the peace process in the Middle East. At the Carter Center he hosted eight Soviet officials who attended a consultation on arms control that the CNN cable network carried for 11 hours. On national TV in Colombia to encourage understanding of the value of polio vaccine, he personally injected the serum in two baby boys. In Accra, Ghana, he opened a Carter Center office developed to help that country become self-sufficient in food production within five years. He and Rosalynn wrote *Everything to Gain: Making the Most of the Rest of Your Life*, a book that enjoyed 10 weeks on *The New York Times* best-seller list. When the Carter Center learned that a drug called Mectizan could control river blindness in Africa, a disease spread in fertile river valleys causing skin lesions and blindness to half the

Rosalynn and Jimmy are active volunteers for Habitat for Humanity, which builds and repairs homes for needy people. (Getty Images)

men over 40 years old, he convinced the pharmaceutical giant Merck to donate as much as was needed for as long as needed.

In May 1986, Jimmy Carter's attention was drawn to Guinea worm, a disease in which a parasite carried in polluted drinking water caused infected abscesses in 10 million people in central Africa, Pakistan, and India. It was the only disease, he learned, that came solely from bad water, and clean wells and filters could eliminate it. Jimmy decided the Carter Center should take on the worldwide job of getting rid of Guinea worm. Using his unique authority as former president, he began talking to heads of state about the disease and making speeches on it wherever he traveled.

Making Elections Work

An election in May 1989 launched another major Carter Center activity. Panama's dictator, General Manuel Noriega, was fighting against a fair and free election. Three organizations in the U.S. sent former presidents Carter and Ford to Panama to head a team to monitor the election. With the Carter team's encouragement to get out and vote, Panamanians in large numbers elected Guillermo Endara.

Next Jimmy went to Nicaragua, where President Daniel Ortega expected to win re-election following a violently bitter campaign. When Jimmy told him the returns showed him losing, Ortega said, "No, it's impossible."

"I can tell you from my own experience," said Jimmy, "that losing is not the end of the world. Your greatest accomplishment as president will be if you lead a peaceful transition of power." He then went to the winner, Violetta Chamorro, and got her to call for national reconciliation. Later, at the United Nations, a Nicaraguan diplomat said, "Jimmy Carter saved my country from civil war."

After that, over the next decade, the Carter Center successfully monitored one national election after another, including the Dominican Republic; Haiti; Surinam; Zambia; Guyana; Ghana; Paraguay; Palestine; Jamaica; Venezuela; Nigeria; Indonesia; Mozambique; Mexico; and even villages in China and the Cherokee Nation in Oklahoma. In some countries, observers noted, only the presence of Jimmy Carter prevented losers from rioting in the streets.

Building Elections and Houses

More than 500 longtime friends and associates gathered in Atlanta on October 1, 1994, to salute Jimmy Carter on his 70th birthday. They celebrated the life achievements of a man whose career in politics—from Georgia legislator through the U.S. presidency—covered only 18 years but who had become known as "the best ex-president in

American history." People agreed that Jimmy Carter had never failed to put principle ahead of politics. In fact, all knew, he had always looked on politics as simply a way to get things done.

That major birthday did not slow down Jimmy Carter. By December, he and Rosalynn were in the former Yugoslavia getting the fighting Bosnian Muslims and Serbs to agree to a four-month cease-fire and peace talks. The next March, in Sudan, Jimmy negotiated a two-month cease-fire between warring tribes and started them getting rid of river blindness and Guinea worm disease as well as immunizing children against polio and other diseases.

At home, Jimmy's wide-ranging talents included writing a children's book, *The Little Baby Snoogle-Fleejer*, based on a bedtime story he had long ago invented for his children. His daughter, Amy, who had now earned her master's degree in art history, drew the illustrations. Then came a special honor on April 27, 1998, when a Navy submarine, the USS *Jimmy Carter*, was christened. It was one of the extremely few Navy vessels ever named for a living person.

On December 10, 1998, the UN celebrated the 50th anniversary of its Universal Declaration of Human Rights by giving Jimmy Carter its first United Nations Human Rights Prize. The next year, President Bill Clinton presented the highest civilian award in the United States, the

Jimmy and Cuban leader Fidel Castro; Jimmy was the first U.S. president to visit the island nation since 1928. (Getty Images)

Presidential Medal of Freedom, to Jimmy and Rosalynn Carter. For the Carters, receiving such awards meant scurrying back and forth among Plains, New York, and Washington while continuing to monitor elections in such lands as Indonesia, Mozambique, or Peru. It also meant saving time for their continuing work with Habitat for Humanity.

In the millenarian year 2000, the Carter Center introduced another major program, called *Global 2000*. To improve living conditions in nearly two dozen poor African countries, it taught ways to improve health, presented new varieties of grain that could double or triple farm production, and developed reforestation plans—all on Jimmy Carter's basic principle that "people can improve their lives when provided with the necessary skills, knowledge, and access to resources."

In May 2002, Jimmy and Rosalynn accepted an invitation from Fidel Castro, president of Cuba, to bring a group there from the Carter Center. No U.S. president, either former or while in office, had visited that island since 1928. In meetings with Castro, he challenged the dictator to introduce democracy there, and on coming home he called for the U.S. to lift the trade embargo that had been in place since the missile crisis in 1962.

Like Theodore Roosevelt and Woodrow Wilson

When Jimmy Carter got the call at 4:30 in the morning telling him he had won the Nobel Peace Prize, he became only the third U.S. president ever to win it. Theodore Roosevelt and Woodrow Wilson had preceded him. For the 2002 prize, the Nobel Committee considered 156 candidates—117 individuals and 39 groups (the list of nominees is kept secret for another 50 years).

Presenting the prize in Oslo, Norway, on December 10, 2002, Gunnar Berge, chairman of the Nobel Committee, said, "This year's Laureate has contributed in practically all the areas that have figured most prominently through the one hundred and one years of Peace Prize history. He was the politician who during his presidency attempted to bring about a more peaceful world. He was, and contin-

Rosalynn and Jimmy at the Democratic National Convention in 2004 (AFP/Getty Images)

ues to be, the mediator who seeks peaceful solutions to international conflicts. He was, and is, engaged in disarmament and arms control. He has shown, and still shows, an outstanding commitment to democracy and human rights. His humanitarian and social activities have been, and are still, far-reaching."

Accepting the award, Jimmy Carter spoke at length. He told his audience how his beloved teacher, Miss Julia Coleman, often said, "We must adjust to changing times and still hold to unchanging principles." Then he went on to say, "This same teacher introduced me to Leo Tolstoy's novel *War and Peace.* She interpreted that powerful narrative as a reminder that the simple human attributes of goodness and truth can overcome great power. She also taught us that an individual is not swept along on a tide of inevitability but can influence even the greatest human events."

TIME LINE

1924	Born October 1 in Plains, Georgia
1928	Family moves to farm in Archery, near Plains
1930	Starts selling peanuts on street in Plains
1933	Buys and stores cotton bales
1937	Sells cotton, buys tenant houses
1941	Represents Plains High School at national Future Farmers of America conventions
1943	Receives appointment to U.S. Naval Academy
1946	Graduates from Naval Academy; marries Rosalynn Smith
1947	Son John William Carter is born
1948	Accepted at six-month submarine officer training school, New London, Connecticut

1949 Assigned to USS *Pomfret* based at Pearl Harbor; nearly swept overboard in storm

1950 Second child, son James Earl Carter III ("Chip") is born

1951 Senior officer of pre-commissioning detail aboard first postwar submarine, the K-1

1952 Accepted in elite nuclear submarine program; third son, Donnel Jeffrey Carter, is born

1953 Father dies of pancreatic cancer; resigns Navy commission, returns to family business in Plains

1963 Defeated in race for Georgia State Senate, demands recount, wins

1966 Loses Democratic primary race for Georgia governorship; long talk with evangelical Christian sister Ruth starts "born again" experience

1967 Daughter, Amy Lynn Carter, is born

1968 Drives to Lock Haven, Pennsylvania, to witness for his faith

1970 Elected governor of Georgia

1971 At inauguration, declares "the time for racial discrimination is over"

1972 At Democratic National Convention, works unsuccessfully to block nomination of George McGovern for president; starts planning to win 1976 nomination

1973 *What's My Line?* panel fails to identify Governor Carter; appointed to Trilateral Commission by David Rockefeller

1974 Announces candidacy for president

1976 Wins primaries and nomination; wins debate with President Gerald Ford; elected president on November 2

1977 In inaugural parade, walks from Capitol to White House; pardons Vietnam draft evaders; delivers "fireside chat" on energy policy; meets Middle East leaders; ends B-1 bomber program; signs Panama Canal treaties; establishes Department of Energy; visits Shah of Iran

1978 Stops production of neutron bomb; invites Egyptian president Sadat and Israeli prime minister Begin to Camp David summit meeting

1979 Travels to Middle East to salvage Camp David agreements, resulting in Sadat and Begin signing historic Egypt-Israel treaty on White House lawn; calms alarmed citizens after atomic power plant meltdown at Three Mile Island; with Soviet premier Brezhnev, signs SALT II arms control agreement in Vienna; meets with advisers at Camp David and adjusts attitude toward micro-management of government; proposes six-point energy plan; permits Shah of Iran to enter U.S. for medical treatment, resulting in militant students in Tehran taking 66 hostages at American embassy

1980 After Soviets invade Afghanistan, recalls ambassador from Moscow and cancels American participation in 1980 Summer Olympics in Moscow; mission to rescue Tehran hostages ends in disaster; wins Democratic nomination for second term; debates Republican candidate Ronald Reagan; loses election; hostages released on Reagan's Inauguration Day

1981 Attends Cairo funeral of assassinated Egyptian president Sadat

1982 Starts planning the Carter Center, "a place to help people resolve disputes"

1984 Joins a Habitat for Humanity construction crew in Americus; building of the Carter Center begins

1985 Administers polio vaccine in Colombia; hosts arms-control consultation with Soviet officials

1986 The Carter Center opens office in Ghana; President Reagan dedicates the Carter Center headquarters in Atlanta

1987 Jimmy and Rosalynn Carter's book *Everything to Gain: Making the Most of the Rest of Your Life*, hits *New York Times* best-seller list; convinces Merck to donate drug Mectizan to control river blindness in Africa

1989 Starts monitoring elections, first in Panama

1990 Convinces Nicaraguan President Ortega to accept defeat; continues monitoring elections worldwide

1991 The Carter Center announces Mental Health Task Force headed by Rosalynn Carter, then announces Atlanta Project to address inner-city social problems

1992 Carters visit African countries to lead effort to wipe out Guinea worm disease

1993 Pakistan announces Guinea worm disease is eradicated

1994 Carters discuss nuclear disarmament with North and South Korean leaders and plan reunification talks; in Haiti, mission restores President Aristide to power following ouster by military junta; in Bosnia and Serbia, mission establishes cease-fire and peace talks

1995 Negotiates Sudan agreement to immunize children and fight both river blindness and Guinea worm disease

1996–1997 Continues monitoring elections worldwide; continues working one week a year for Habitat for Humanity

1998 Observes village elections in China and advises Chinese government on elections; receives first UN Human Rights Prize

1999 Receives Presidential Medal of Freedom

2000 Introduces *Global 2000* to improve living conditions in nearly two dozen poor African countries

2002 Visits Cuba and calls on U.S. to lift trade embargo; receives Nobel Peace Prize

2004 Makes major speech at Democratic National Convention; celebrates 80th birthday

HOW TO BECOME A FEDERAL OR STATE OFFICIAL

THE JOB

Think about the last time you cast a vote, whether in a school, local, state, or federal election. How did you make your decision? Was it based on the personal qualities of the candidate? The political positions of the candidate? Certain issues of importance to you? Or do you always vote for the same political party? As voters, we choose carefully when electing a government official, taking many different things into consideration. Whether you're electing a new governor and lieutenant governor for the state, a president and vice president for the country, or senators and representatives for the state legislature or the U.S. Congress, you're choosing people to act on behalf of your interests. The decisions of state and federal lawmakers affect your daily life and your future. State and federal officials pass laws concerning the arts, education, taxes, employment, healthcare, and other areas, in efforts to change and improve communities and standards of living.

Besides the president and vice president of the United States, the executive branch of the national government consists of the president's Cabinet, including, among others, the secretaries of state, treasury, defense, interior, agriculture, homeland security, and health and human services. These officials are appointed by the president and approved by the Senate. The members of the Office of Management and Budget, the Council of Economic Advisors, and the National Security Council are also executive officers of the national government.

Nearly every state's governing body resembles that of the federal government. Just as the U.S. Congress is composed of the Senate and the House of Representatives, so does each state (with one exception, Nebraska) have a senate and a house. The executive branch of the U.S. government is headed by the president and vice president, while the states elect governors and lieutenant governors. The *governor* is the chief executive officer of a state. In all states, a large government administration handles a variety of functions related to agriculture, highway and motor vehicle supervision, public safety and corrections, regulation of intrastate business and industry, and some aspects of education, public health, and welfare. The governor's job is to manage this administration. Some states also have a lieutenant governor, who serves as the presiding officer of the state's senate. Other elected officials commonly include a secretary of state, state treasurer, state auditor, attorney general, and superintendent of public instruction.

State senators and state representatives are the legislators elected to represent the districts and regions of cities and counties within the state. The number of members of a state's legislature varies from state to state. In the U.S. Congress, there are 100 senators (as established by the Constitution—two senators from each state) and 435 representatives. The number of representatives each state is allowed to send to the U.S. Congress varies based on the state's population as determined by the national census. Based on results from Census 2000, California is the most populous state and sends the most representatives (53). The primary function of all legislators, on both the state and national levels, is to make laws. With a staff of aides, senators and representatives attempt to learn as much as they can about the bills being considered. They research legislation, prepare reports, meet with constituents and interest groups, speak to the press, and discuss and debate legislation on the floor of the House or Senate. Legislators also may be involved in selecting other members of the government, supervising the government administration, appropriating funds, impeaching executive and judicial officials, and determining election procedures, among other activities. A state legislator may be involved in examining such situations as the state's relationship to Native American tribes, the level of school violence, and welfare reform.

"Time in each day goes by so quickly," says Don Preister, who serves on the state legislature in Nebraska, "there's no time to read up on all legislation and all the information the constituents send in." The state of Nebraska is the only state with a single-house system. When the state senate is in session, Preister commits many hours to discussing and debating issues with other state senators and gathering information on proposed legislation. In addition to senate sessions, Preister attends committee hearings. His committees include Natural Resources and Urban Affairs. "A hearing lasts from 20 minutes to three or four hours," he says, "depending on the intensity of the issues." Despite having to devote about 60 hours a week to the job when the senate is in session, Preister finds his work a wonderful opportunity to be of service to the community and to improve lives. "I take a lot of personal satisfaction from being a voice for people whose voices aren't often heard in government."

REQUIREMENTS

High School

Courses in government, civics, and history will give you an understanding of the structure of state and federal governments. English courses are important because you need good writing skills for communicating with constituents and other government officials. Math and accounting help you to develop the analytical skills needed for examining statistics and demographics. You should take science courses because you'll be making decisions concerning health, medicine, and technological advances. Journalism classes will help you learn about the print and broadcast media and the role they play in politics. Take public speaking courses, as communicating verbally is fundamental to a career as a public official.

Postsecondary Training

State and federal legislators come from all walks of life. Some hold master's degrees and doctorates, while others have only a high school education. Although a majority of government officials hold law degrees, others have undergraduate or graduate degrees in such areas as journalism, economics, political science, history, and English. Regardless of your major as an undergraduate, it is important to take classes in English literature, statistics, foreign language, Western civilization, and economics. Graduate studies can focus more on one area of study; some prospective government officials pursue master's degrees in public administration or international affairs. Consider participating in an internship program that will involve you with local and state officials. Contact the offices of your state legislators and of your state's members of Congress to apply for internships directly.

Other Requirements

"You should have concern for people," Don Preister says. "You should have an ability to listen and understand people and their concerns." This attention to the needs of communities should be of foremost importance to anyone pursuing a government office. Although historically some politicians have had questionable purposes in their campaigns for office, most successful politicians are devoted to making positive changes and improvements. Good people skills will help you make connections, get elected, and make things happen once in office. You should also enjoy public speaking, argument, debate, and opposition—you'll get a lot of it as you attempt to get laws passed.

A good temperament in such situations will earn you the respect of your colleagues. Strong character and a good background will help you to avoid the personal attacks that occasionally accompany government office.

EXPLORING

If you are 16 or older, you can gain experience in a legislature. The U.S. Congress and possibly your state legislature offer opportunities for young adults who have demonstrated a commitment to government study to work as pages. For Congress, pages run messages across Capitol Hill, and have the opportunity to see senators and representatives debating and discussing bills. The length of a page's service can be for one summer or up to one year. Contact your state's senator or representative for an application.

You can also explore government careers by becoming involved with local elections. Many candidates for local and state offices welcome young people to assist with campaigns. You might be asked to make calls, post signs, or hand out information about the candidate. Not only will you get to see the politician at work, but you will also meet others with an interest in government.

Another great way to learn about government is to become involved in an issue of interest to you. Participate with a grassroots advocacy group or read about the bills up for vote in the state legislature and U.S. Congress. When you feel strongly about an issue and are well educated on the subject, contact the offices of state legislators and members of Congress to express your views. Visit the websites of the House and Senate and of your state legislature to read about bills, schedules, and the legislators. The National Conference of State Legislators (NCSL) also hosts a website (http://www.ncsl.org) featuring legislative news and links to state legislatures.

EMPLOYERS

State legislators work for the state government, and many hold other jobs as well. Because of the part-time nature of some legislative offices, state legislators may hold part-time jobs or own their own businesses. Federal officials work full time for the Senate, the House, or the executive branch.

STARTING OUT

There is no direct career path for state and federal officials. Some enter into their positions after some success with political activism on the grassroots level. Others work their way up from local government positions to state legislature and into federal office. Those who serve as U.S. Congress members have worked in the military, journalism, academics, business, and many other fields.

Many politicians get their start assisting someone else's campaign or advocating for an issue. Don Preister's beginnings with the Nebraska state legislature are particularly inspiring. Because of his involvement in grassroots organizing to improve his neighborhood, he was encouraged by friends and neighbors to run for senator of the district. Others, however, believed he'd never get elected running against a man who'd had a lot of political success, as well as great finances to back his campaign. "I didn't have any money," Preister says, "or any experience in campaigning. So I went door to door to meet the people of the district. I went to every house and apartment in the district." He won that election in 1992 and won again in 1996 and 2000.

ADVANCEMENT

Initiative is one key to success in politics. Advancement can be rapid for someone who is a fast learner and is independently motivated, but a career in politics most often takes a long time to establish. Most state and federal officials start by pursuing training and work experience in their particular field, while getting involved in politics at the local level. Many people progress from local politics to state politics. It is not uncommon for a state legislator to eventually run for a seat in Congress. Appointees to the president's Cabinet and presidential and vice presidential candidates frequently have held positions in Congress.

EARNINGS

In general, salaries for government officials tend to be lower than what the official could make working in the private sector. In the case of state legislators, the pay can be very much lower.

The Bureau of Labor Statistics reports that the median annual earnings of government legislators were $15,220 in 2002. Salaries generally ranged from less than $12,130 to more than $69,380, although some officials earn nothing at all.

According to the NCSL, state legislators make from $10,000 to $65,000 a year. A few states, however, don't pay state legislators anything but an expense allowance. But a state's executive officials get paid better: Salaries of state governors range from $86,000 in Alaska to a high of $179,000 in New York.

In 2004, U.S. senators and representatives earned $158,000; the vice president was paid $202,900; and the president earned $400,000.

Congressional leaders such as the Speaker of the House and the Senate majority leader receive higher salaries than the other Congress members. The Speaker of the House makes $202,900 a year. U.S. Congress members receive excellent insurance, vacation, and other benefits.

WORK ENVIRONMENT

Most government officials work in a typical office setting. Some may work a regular 40-hour week, while others will typically work long hours and weekends. One potential drawback to political life, particularly for the candidate running for office, is that there is no real off-duty time. One is continually under observation by the press and public, and the personal lives of candidates and office-holders are discussed frequently in the media.

Because these officials must be appointed or elected in order to keep their jobs, the ability to determine long-range job objectives is slim. There may be extended periods of unemployment, when living off of savings or working at other jobs may be necessary.

Frequent travel is involved in campaigning and in holding office, so some people with children may find the lifestyle demanding on their families.

OUTLOOK

The U.S. Department of Labor predicts that employment of federal and state officials will grow about as fast as the average through 2012. To attract more candidates to run for legislative offices, states may consider salary increases and better benefits for state senators and representatives. But changes in pay and benefits for federal officials are unlikely. An increase in the number of representatives is possible as the U.S. population grows, but would require additional office space and other costly expansions. For the most part, the structures of state and federal legislatures will remain unchanged, although the topic of limiting the number of terms that a representative is allowed to serve does often arise in election years.

The federal government has made efforts to shift costs to the states; if this continues, it could change the way state legislatures and executive officers operate with regard to public funding. Already, welfare reform has resulted in state governments looking for financial aid in handling welfare cases and job programs. Arts funding may also become the sole responsibility of the states as programs such as the National Endowment for the Arts lose support from Congress.

With the government's commitment to developing a place on the Internet, contacting your state and federal representatives, learning about legislation, and organizing grassroots advocacy have become much easier. This voter awareness of candidates, public policy issues, and legislation will increase and may affect how future representatives make decisions. Also look for government programming to be part of cable television's expansion into digital broadcasting. New modes of communication will allow constituents to become even more involved in the actions of their representatives.

TO LEARN MORE ABOUT FEDERAL AND STATE OFFICIALS

BOOKS

Dye, Thomas R., and Susan A. MacManus. *Politics in States and Communities.* 11th ed. Upper Saddle River, N.J.: Prentice Hall, 2002.

Kennedy, John F. *Profiles in Courage.* New York: HarperCollins, 2003.

Lewis, Barbara A. *The Kid's Guide to Service Projects: Over 500 Service Projects for Young People Who Want to Make a Difference.* Minneapolis: Free Spirit, 1995.

Sobel, Syl. *How the U.S. Government Works.* Hauppauge, N.Y.: Barron's, 1999.

———. *Presidential Elections and Other Cool Facts.* 2d ed. Hauppauge, N.Y.: Barron's, 2001.

ORGANIZATIONS AND WEBSITES

Visit the Senate and House websites for extensive information about Congress, government history, current legislation, and links to state legislature sites. To inquire about internship opportunities with your Congress member, contact

U.S. Senate
Office of Senator (Name)
United States Senate
Washington, DC 20510
Tel: 202-224-3121
http://www.senate.gov

U.S. House of Representatives
Office of the Honorable (Name)
Washington, DC 20515
Tel: 202-224-3121
http://www.house.gov

To read about state legislatures, policy issues, legislative news, and other related information, visit the NCSL's website.

National Conference of State Legislatures (NCSL)
444 North Capitol Street, NW, Suite 515
Washington, DC 20001
Tel: 202-624-5400
Email: info@ncsl.org
http://www.ncsl.org

TO LEARN MORE ABOUT JIMMY CARTER

BOOKS AND ARTICLES

Adler, Bill. *The Wit and Wisdom of Jimmy Carter*. Secaucus, N.J.: Citadel Press, 1977.

Baker, James T. *A Southern Baptist in the White House*. Philadelphia: Westminster Press, 1977.

Bartley, Numan V. *Jimmy Carter and the Politics of the New South*. St. Louis: Forum Press, 1979.

Beschloss, Michael. "Debating Your Way to Defeat." *The New York Times*, October 17, 2004.

Bourne, Peter G. *Jimmy Carter: A Comprehensive Biography from Plains to Postpresidency*. New York: A Lisa Drew Book/Scribner, 1997.

Brinkley, Douglas. *The Unfinished Presidency: Jimmy Carter's Journey Beyond the White House*. New York: Viking, 1998.

Byrd, Max. "Founding Bubbas." *The New York Times Book Review*, November 23, 2003.

Callaghan, Dorothy. *Jimmy, the Story of the Young Jimmy Carter*. Garden City, N.Y.: Doubleday, 1979.

Carter, Jimmy. *Why Not the Best?* Nashville: Broadman Press, 1975.

———. *A Government as Good as Its People*. New York: Simon & Schuster, 1978.

———. *Keeping Faith: Memoirs of a President*. New York: Bantam Books, 1982.

———. *The Blood of Abraham: Insights into the Middle East*. Boston: Houghton Mifflin, 1986.

———. *An Outdoor Journal: Adventures and Reflections*. New York: Bantam Books, 1988.

———. *Turning Point: A Candidate, a State, and a Nation Come of Age*. New York: Times Books, 1992.

———. *Talking Peace: A Vision for the Next Generation*. New York: Dutton Children's Books, 1993.

———. *Always a Reckoning, and Other Poems*. New York: Times Books, 1995.

——. *Living Faith*. New York: Times Books, 1996.

——. Illus. by Amy Carter. *The Little Baby Snoogle-Fleejer*. New York: Times Books, 1996.

——. *The Virtues of Aging*. New York: Ballantine Books, 1998.

——. *Sources of Strength: Meditations on Scripture for a Living Faith*. New York: Crown (Three Rivers Press), 1999.

——. *An Hour Before Daylight*. New York: Simon & Schuster, 2001.

——. *Christmas in Plains*. New York: Simon & Schuster, 2001.

——. *The Hornet's Nest: A Novel of the Revolutionary War*. New York: Simon & Schuster, 2003.

Carter, Jimmy, and Rosalynn Carter. *Everything to Gain: Making the Most of the Rest of Your Life*. New York: Random House, 1987.

Carter, Rosalynn. *First Lady from Plains*. New York: Ballantine Books, 1984.

Fuller, Millard. *No More Shacks: The Daring Vision of Habitat for Humanity*. Waco, Tex.: Word Books, 1986.

Glad, Betty. *Jimmy Carter, in Search of the Great White House*. New York: Norton, 1980.

Isaacs, Harold. *Jimmy Carter's Peanut Brigade*. Dallas, Tex.: Taylor Publishing Company, 1977.

Jordan, Hamilton. *The Last Year of the Carter Presidency*. New York: G.P. Putnam's Sons, 1982.

Lance, Bert. *The Truth of the Matter*. New York: Summit Books, 1991.

Lasky, Victor. *Jimmy Carter, the Man and the Myth*. New York: R. Marek, 1979.

Miller, William L. *Yankee from Georgia: The Emergence of Jimmy Carter*. New York: Times Books, 1978.

Mollenhoff, Clark R. *The President Who Failed*. New York: Macmillan, 1980.

Morris, Kenneth E. *Jimmy Carter: American Moralist*. Athens, Ga.: The University of Georgia Press, 1996.

Powell, Jody. *The Other Side of the Story*. New York: Morrow, 1984.

Sick, Gary. *The October Surprise: America's Hostages in Iran and the Election of Ronald Reagan*. New York: Times Books, 1991.

INTERNET SOURCES

"POTUS: Presidents of the United States: James Earl Carter, Jr." Internet Public Library website. Available online. http://www.ipl.org/div/potus/jecarter.html. Downloaded September 17, 2004.

"Jimmy Carter." White House website. Available online. http://www.whitehouse.gov/history/presidents/text/jc39.html. Downloaded September 17, 2004.

"Jimmy Carter." Wikipedia, the free encyclopedia website. Available online. http://en.wikipedia.org/wiki/Jimmy_Carter. Downloaded September 17, 2004.

"Jimmy Carter." Character Above All Essays website. Available online. http://www.pbs.org/newshour/character/essays/carter.html. Downloaded September 17, 2004.

"About Us." The Carter Center website. Available online. http://www.cartercenter.org/aboutus/aboutus.html. Downloaded September 17, 2004.

"General Information." Jimmy Carter Library & Museum website. Available online. http://www.jimmycarterlibrary.gov/information/. Downloaded September 17, 2004.

"Jimmy Carter National Historic Site." National Park Service website. Available online. http://www.nps.gov/jica/. Downloaded September 17, 2004.

"Jimmy Carter and Habitat." Habitat for Humanity International website. Available online. http://www.

habitat.org/how/carter.html. Downloaded September 17, 2004.

"Jimmy Carter wins Nobel Peace Prize." CNN.com website, October 11, 2002. Available online. http://archives.cnn.com/2002/WORLD/europe/10/11/carter.nobel. Downloaded September 17, 2004.

"Presentation Speech—2002 Nobel Peace Prize Award." Nobelprize.org website. Available online. http://nobelprize.org/cgi-bin/print?from=/peace/laureates/2002/presentation-speech.html. Downloaded September 17, 2004.

"Jimmy Carter—Nobel Lecture." Nobelprize.org website. Available online. http://nobelprize.org/cgi-bin/print?from=/peace/laureates/2002/carter-lecture.html. Downloaded September 17, 2004.

"Jimmy Carter celebrates 80th birthday Friday." Yahoo News website, September 30, 2004. Available online. http://news.yahoo.com/. Downloaded September 30, 2004.

"What is a neutron bomb?" Manuelsweb.com website. Available online. http://www.manuelsweb.com/neutronbomb.htm. Downloaded October 19, 2004.

"Helsinki Accords." Wikipedia, the free encyclopedia website. Available online. http://en.wikipedia.org/wiki/Helsinki_Accords. Downloaded November 1, 2004.

"SALT II." Wikipedia, the free encyclopedia website. Available online. http://en.wikipedia.org/wiki/SALT_II. Downloaded November 1, 2004.

"Anwar al-Sadat." Internet Bibliographies website. Available online. http://www.ibiblio.org/sullivan/bios/Sadat-bio.html. Downloaded November 1, 2004.

"Onchocerciasis (river blindness)—disease information." World Health Organization website. Available online. http://www.who.int/pbd/blindness/onchocerciasis/disease/en/print.html. Downloaded November 1, 2004.

INDEX

Page numbers in *italics* indicate illustrations.

ABOUT THE AUTHOR

Bernard Ryan, Jr., has authored, co-authored, or ghost-written 34 books in such topics as biography, early childhood education, community service for teens, career guides in the fields of advertising and journalism, courtroom trials, and personal financial planning, including five in the Ferguson Career Biographies series: *Condoleezza Rice: Secretary of State*; *Hillary Rodham Clinton: First Lady and Senator*; *Stephen Hawking: Physicist and Educator*; *Jeff Bezos: Business Executive and Founder of Amazon.com*; and *Warren Buffett: Financier*. His *Tyler's Titanic* is an early chapter book about what happens when a boy finds a way to visit the wreckage of the great ship on the ocean floor. In *The Wright Brothers: Inventors of the Airplane*, he tells the sixth- to ninth-grade reader the Wrights' life stories and explains how they brought the world the miracle of flight. His *Helping Your Child Start School* is an introduction to kindergarten for parents. *Simple Ways to Help Your Kids Become Dollar-Smart*, co-authored with financial planner Elizabeth Lewin, helps parents teach children ages seven to 18 how to handle money. His *The Poisoned Life of Mrs. Maybrick* is the biography of an American woman who, in Liverpool, England, in 1889, was the defendant in one of history's great murder trials. Mr. Ryan has written many shorter pieces for magazine and newspaper publication and is a graduate of The Rectory School, Kent School, and Princeton University. A native of Albion, New York, he lives with his wife, Jean Bramwell Ryan, in Southbury, Connecticut. They have two daughters and two grandchildren.